last to Leave Home

Our Special Brother
Their Special Child

Carolyn S. Baker, EdD

Published 2007 by Mark's Sunshine, LLC.
Nashville, Tennessee
2nd edition, 2008

ISBN 978-0-9791784-0-5

Original cover design by David Read, Nashville, Tennessee

Professional photo contributions:
Raj Natarajan - Houston, Texas
Larry Haney, Haney Whipple Portraits, Houston, Texas
(author photograph)

Editor- Kendal Gladish
Designer- Layne Moore

Last To Leave Home can be purchased for
business or promotional purposes.
For more information, please contact:
Carolyn Baker
1616 Fountain View Dr.
Suite 403
Houston, TX 77057
832-252-7334
Or email carolynbaker@sbcglobal.net

Proceeds from the sale of this book will be donated to The
Adult Down Syndrome Center in Atlanta, Georgia.

Printed and bound in The United States of America by Morris
Printing Services.

In honor of Mark

who touched so many with
his unconditional love

Dedicated to Dianna

Mark's special sister
and my dearest friend

And To
Mom and Dad

Your choice to keep Mark at home made all the difference
along with your continual love and support

Mark and his parents walk from the mailbox at this home in Virginia.

Table of Contents
(Chapter titles are my brother's well known mantras)

Foreward
Prologue
Introduction

Part I - My Brother's Adult Years Begin

Hi! I'm Mark Simpson
Call the Sheriff
I Can Do That
All That Crap
I 'member That
I Want Sunshine
I DID NOT! I Didn't Do It!
I Appreciate That
Gimme a Job

Part II - Am I My Brother's Keeper?

I Go With You
I Love Camp
Goin to Nashville
Now You Tell Me!
I'm So Upset
I Need a Haircut
McDonalds
Steve and Nancy

Part III - I AM My Brother's Keeper!

Thank God, I'm a Country Boy
I Stay Right Here
Th-h-h-ank You
It's About Time
You're My Sister
Let Us Pray

Foreward

Ring the bells that still can ring
Forget your perfect offering
There is a crack in everything
That's how the light gets in.

We asked for signs
the signs were sent:

Ring the bells that still can ring
Forget your perfect offering
There is a crack, a crack in everything
That's how the light gets in.
That's how the light gets in.
That's how the light gets in.

This is a book about a family. A good family, who live together, grow up together, laugh together and cry together. This book is about their pain and their passion, their struggles and their successes but most of all it is about their love. Not a one-dimensional made-for-the public love, but complex love with challenges and difficult choices, with growth and changes with understanding and misunderstanding – in fact this is a book about a real family told in real language about real life events and vignettes. We get to see the many aspects of many family members told in brief thematic quanta, much like a collection of short stories strung together in a chronological sequence. The mode of short story telling gives the book a multifaceted approach and appeal that comes together very nicely and serves to construct a form of family mini-saga.

This is a story about a family of 7 children one of whom happens to have Down syndrome and is the focal point of the book. Mark is the son who is the *Last to Leave Home*; he is the central character and protagonist in this family saga which is told by his big sister. She begins the book with an emotionally searing vignette when she as a big sister sets out to help her little brother to learn to read. The lessons she learns are painful but she learns to understand her brother and herself much better through the exercise. This theme of learning from her brother rather than teaching him runs throughout the book and is probably the most significant aspect that reaches and touches the whole family. As is often said, children do not come with instruction manuals and children who have Down syndrome would require instruction manuals that are more like telephone books than brochures. Although today we have the benefit of years of documented experience and research in child rearing and even in rearing children who have Down syndrome, when Mark was a little boy in the 1950's there was not much known or documented that was supportive or proactive let alone therapeutic or educational. At the time, the choice given to parents was not uncommonly that they should place their child in a residential setting and get on with their lives. Obviously Mark's parents had the conviction and made the commitment to keep Mark at home with them and love him and treat him like any of their other children; this sets in motion the rich and raw lessons that they all learned from Mark and from each other and what Mrs. Baker has captured for us to learn.

For families who have children with Down syndrome today, there are a plethora of services and supports, research and literature on the health, growth, development and education of infants and children with this condition. There is also extensive and increasing understanding of family dynamics and of social adaptation and acceptance that is available to families. There are books and TV shows and movies; there are associations and conferences and national organizations; there are employment opportunities, college opportunities, social and personal relationships, and special lifecycle events like Confirmations, Bar mitzvahs and even weddings. The lives of individuals with Down syndrome and their families today are very different from the world that Mrs. Baker portrays. The world of Mark's family is one of a pioneering spirit, of strong willed, determined, stout hearted loving and caring people who are willing to make personal sacrifices for the good of the family.

Mark thrived, he grew, he developed, he participated fully in all family events; he worked and loved it, he had a sense of humor and he had his passions. He was a regular guy among regular guys. His family supported and nurtured his potential and he used his strengths fully and constructively and was proud of it. Like all of us, he had insights and sensitivities that gave him both his strength of character and his vulnerability. The book does not spare us his pain nor his sense of pride and determination and in so doing, he emerges as a real hero.

In life, it is tough to grow old, and this is where his parents are getting older and his siblings are old enough to leave home, while Mark has to remain – *The Last to Leave Home*. Also as age takes its toll on Mark with limitations in his activity and work, it also confers on him medical illnesses and conditions that are associated with aging. Here his siblings come together again to help organize their parents and give Mark the opportunity to leave home and we learn that he values this and the independence that it brings.

Unfortunately this phase of his life – the phase that he had wanted for so long – was short-lived. The aging of his body and the medical complications that ensued began to take over and complicate and compromise his freedom. He began to enter the world of doctors and medicines and hospitals and procedures that would serve to improve his health and reverse as much as possible the aging process of the body's organ systems. These medical complications are what had brought me into contact with Mark and his family and his deeply dedicated physician Dr. Stewart Sharp, with whom I shared many phone calls and discussions about his medical management.

Unfortunately, all efforts to reverse the medical complications of aging could not change the course of events and Mark passed away within months of our meeting. The letters and speeches by Mark's family of his generation and of the next generation speak to the love and caring that he engendered and that was such a vital part of the family collective spirit.

From 1980 to 1994 I had the opportunity and privilege to work in the Down Syndrome Infant Follow Up Clinic that Sig Peuschell and Allen Crocker started at The Children's Hospital in Boston. I had the pleasure of working with creative, talented and dedicated professionals who were part of the interdisciplinary team of the Developmental Evaluation Clinic who not only evaluated the children and their families but who also understood what they were doing and shared their accumulated knowledge and understanding with others and in so doing changed the way we see infants and children with Down syndrome today. Most significantly, I had the wonderful opportunity to see the little infants (some very soon after birth) and watch them grow and develop not only physically and cognitively but to see their personalities unfold. I had the privilege and opportunity to meet their parents, their brothers and sisters and on occasion their extended family members. I watched and learned and many of my most valuable lessons were from the parents and families. The most memorable one was – *I used to be worried about what my child could not do, but now I celebrate everything that my child can do.*

After 14 years at the Boston Children's Hospital I moved to Atlanta, Georgia. Once again I had the privilege and opportunity to encounter some people who helped to shape the landscape of understanding and appreciation for children and adults with Down syndrome and who have pioneered many services that are currently available in Atlanta today. They were mainly mothers and fathers who were not satisfied with what their children were not getting and took the matter into their own hands and created programs and services and raised awareness among families, professionals and policy makers that continue to this day. One of these parents is Janice Nodvin whose son was born 25 years ago. She has relentlessly worked at a personal and professional level to make sure that her son and his peers have all the opportunities that society has to offer and more. Janice has a professional background in education and because of her professional background and personal circumstances she was hired as the Parent Advocate for the Marcus Center at Emory University where I first met her in 1994 when I came to Atlanta.

In 2002, Arthur Dalton contacted me to become part of a multicenter international project on the study of Vitamin E and Alzheimer's disease. For a while Janice and I struggled to develop a clinical partnership that would become the basis for recruitment of individuals with Down syndrome over the age of 50 years to participate in the project. She then suggested that we start our own Down syndrome clinic and submitted a proposal to the Down Syndrome Association of Atlanta which has funded our Down Syndrome Adult Program for the past three years. During this time we have had the honor to meet many older individuals who have Down syndrome and their families and have learned first hand, not only about the clinical condition and its associated challenges, but also the challenges to the families as the aging process and its associated medical, psychological, sociological and spiritual components take their inexorable course.

One such family who came into our lives was the family of Mark Simpson. Mrs. Baker, Mark's sister and the author of the family saga, *Last to Leave Home*, captures the setting and the ambience that we wanted to create and make people feel comfortable as we tried to tackle the difficult and complex task of sorting out the medical, physical, psychological, sociological and spiritual aspects of the lives of the individuals and their families. We were quite amazed and humbled that Mrs. Baker flew all the way form Texas and her sister drove to Atlanta from Virginia to see us and in the book she describes our modest office space and our style and approach. We work as a team, no one person can do everything and as one mother of a child who had cerebral palsy once remarked – *If it takes a village to raise a child, it takes a metropolitan area to raise a child with developmental disabilities*. While not everyone lives in metropolitan areas the principle is that we are not alone, we are interdependent, our human status confers on us the condition of living in families and communities and helping and supporting each other so that inevitably we all benefit from each other in ways we may not even realize and may never even know. In her book, Mrs. Baker captures this with a wonderful and comfortable ease and shares with us the lessons learned through her own experiences and through the experiences of her family and community. This chronicle serves as a rich set of lessons for all of us at many levels and not only provides some practical thoughts and experiential guidelines for many other families, but more importantly provides the personal and spiritual framework for how we deal with the unexpected. Leonard Cohen's song poem that is quoted above exemplifies the notion that our imperfections are what allow the light to shine through. Let there be Light!

Leslie Rubin MD
President, Institute for the Study of Disadvantage and Disability
Medical Director, TEAM Centers and Developmental Pediatrics Specialists
Medical Director, Adult Down Syndrome Program
Visiting Scholar, Department of Pediatrics
Morehouse School of Medicine
Atlanta, Georgia

November 5, 2006

Mark enjoys a visit with his parents at the farm.

Prologue

I am writing this book for those who live with or come in contact with adults who have special needs. My brother Mark, who died in the spring of 2006, touched the lives of those he met. He was funny, good natured (although very stubborn at times), affectionate, and loved to have a good time.

Understanding the unique characteristics of any condition, whether it be Down syndrome, autism, or the myriad of other developmental disabilities, is critical. Education takes away ignorance, allowing tolerance and understanding to come forth. I didn't always have that tolerance. If only I had educated myself about Mark's capacities and his limitations, I would have avoided an experience I regret to this day.

It happened one summer day when I was 13 years old and my brother Mark was 9. I decided to teach him the alphabet. I'm sure I took this on as a challenge. Perhaps someone had made a comment that he could never learn. As an 8th grader, I didn't think about doing research on children with Down syndrome, nor was there much available. I just wanted to help.

I took him to a quiet area. His shared bedroom with bunk beds became our classroom and here is where we sat, on the bottom bunk with flash cards. I was pleased with Mark's response the first day. He seemed to remember several letters as we practiced repetitively.

"Yes, Mark, that's great!" I applauded him. At this rate, I imagined that by the end of the week I could show off my prize student to our family as he would know ALL the letters!

The problem came the next day. As we worked again, I was astonished to find he didn't know any of the letters of the previous day. "He's just not trying," I thought. "I know he can do this as he did so well yesterday."

We repeated the same process, but somehow Mark was not getting the concept. He seemed lost.

"You are not trying, Mark, watch again," I said, my voice rising and teeth gritting.

As he stumbled over letters, I found myself becoming more and more agitated, more impatient. He didn't seem to care, and I was taking all this time for HIM.

The next time he made a mistake, I slapped him across the face.

"MARK, I SAID TO LOOK AT THIS LETTER, IT IS A "B", A "B" LIKE IN BOY."

I hit him again. I remember he cried. I know I gave up. I did not know that this is a characteristic of children with Down Syndrome. He might know something one day, and the next minute, the brain somehow disconnects.

Who was I really trying to help, him or me? After all these years I still get emotional about my mistreatment of my brother that day. I am ashamed of my younger self. I hurt an innocent child... a child who was special and WAS trying to learn. In all my 30 years in education, I have always supported outlawing corporal punishment in schools. It makes me angry at myself that I would treat my own brother in such a way.

I remember a clergyman who said, "Let us ask forgiveness for those we have offended, why is it that we always hurt those we love the most?"

After this incident, I began to realize that although Mark had limitations in learning, he had other gifts. I began to focus on Mark's strengths. His wonderful sense of humor and irresistible personality made us laugh. He worked diligently at the most mundane of tasks. His perseverance was to be admired. He loved being with his siblings and was content to do whatever activity in which we were engaged. His unconditional love was admired by the entire family.

This book is from my point of view, the eldest child of the seven Simpson children. If my brothers and sister wrote a book about Mark, it would be an entire different set of stories and perceptions. My family or any of my brother's caregivers may not agree with my perspective of Mark's life, but one thing we have in common is that we all loved Mark and cared for him deeply.

Last to Leave Home is like a supplemental text with heart. Each chapter chronicles a moment to remember in my brother's life, and is wrapped in tidbits of research or information about Down syndrome (or those with special needs) from respected resources. The book focuses on my brother's adult years with his family living on our farm in Virginia and his journey to his new life in a nearby group home. The treasury of stories has a common thread woven throughout... the thread of love that prevails amid the challenges for parents and siblings when dealing with an adult with special needs.

The book is divided into three parts. Part I, "My Brother's Adult Years Begin" includes stories of Mark and his life on the family farm. The family moved to the farm when Mark was seventeen and he lived there for thirty-two years. Part II, "Am I My Brother's Keeper?" relates my brother's adventures when he stayed with various siblings. Most stories took place when Mark visited my home during summer teaching breaks. Each sibling made an effort to house Mark for a few weeks now and then to give my parents respites from the constant care-giving that my brother required. Part III, "I AM My Brother's Keeper" recounts the events leading up to my brother leaving home in 2001 and the continuing saga of Mark's experiences at the group home. The narrative describes the burden that was thrust upon Mark's siblings (and one we readily accepted)— the burden of finding a suitable home for Mark AND the ongoing involvement with our brother's care. We realized that to stay connected to Mark wherever he lived, we needed to help be "his keeper." This book sheds light on the continual efforts made by family and community service caregivers to give Mark a quality life. There were conflicts, but with perseverance came resolution.

Shortly after I had sent the manuscript for *Last to Leave Home* to my editor, my brother's health deteriorated, resulting in his death in April 2006. I added an Epilogue to share "the rest of the story" with my audience. As difficult as it was to write, the journey helped with my overwhelming sorrow. The Appendix contains advice for siblings who live far from their loved one with special needs as well as those living close. Included are recommendations for websites and books that might be of interest to those wanting ideas for resources and current news in the area of Down syndrome.

I rejoice at the progress that has been made for those with Down syndrome. The early interventions have helped children learn to read and write. Today adults with Down syndrome have jobs and some live on their own. A few are even married. Families with Down syndrome have many avenues to go to for insight and information. There are even web sites explicitly for people with Down syndrome. I am somewhat saddened that our family did not have such resources, but heartened for those who now have so many opportunities.

One has to relax and accept people with special needs just as they are and try to understand that they simply look at life from a different perspective. I hope this book helps those who read it embrace those who are different. Spend some time with people who are "special" and you will find that your own lives will be richer for the experience.

Although Mark was the last to leave home, he is first in our hearts.

Mark did not walk until he was four years old (the doctors said he would NEVER walk). In this photo he is beginning to take his first steps. I was coming home from school and Mark was excited to greet me. In the top photo I am encouraging him to walk to me. In the second photo I hug him and praise his accomplishment.

The first four children -- Mark sits with his sisters and brother, Steve.

Down syndrome is a genetic condition that causes delays in physical and intellectual development. It occurs in approximately one in every 800 live births. Individuals with Down syndrome have 47 chromosomes instead of the usual 46. It is the most frequently occurring chromosomal disorder. Down syndrome is not related to race, nationality, religion or socioeconomic status. The most important fact to know about individuals with Down syndrome is that they are more like others than they are different.

"Facts About Down Syndrome," National Association for Down Syndrome.
Accessed online at www.nads.org, April 23, 2005.
Reprinted with permission

Introduction

The Irish poet and novelist James Stephens said, "What the heart knows today the head will understand tomorrow." My parents knew in their hearts that Mark would thrive in a family atmosphere. Their heads understood little about the condition. Their understanding came day by day as they grew to understand Mark's limitations.

There was very little known about Down syndrome in the 1950's. Misinformation that might have limited my brother's abilities was in wide circulation. Had they paid attention, my parents would not have encouraged Mark to do much, greatly restricting the richness of his life.

My mother recalls vividly Mark's birth.

"Oh, look, Mark is my little Chinese baby," my mother smiled as she spoke with the staff at the hospital after having delivered her fourth child, a second son, on April 23, 1952. Ruth and Carroll Simpson would ultimately welcome seven children into the world.   I was the eldest, senior by only thirteen months to my sister, Dianna.

"When is your husband coming?" the doctor asked matter-of-factly.

Realizing that he would be off duty when my father arrived after work, the doctor made no further comment.

So my mother took her precious bundle home content to have a little boy whose eyes looked a bit slanted. Uninformed about his condition, she took him into her arms, loving him from the moment he was born. Mom would have always loved Mark regardless, but no hospital today would discharge a mother and baby with Down syndrome without disclosing the facts.

I'm sure the faces of the nurses and doctor must have hinted that something was amiss. I'm sure the doctor was waiting for the right time to share his news.

I'm sure my mother was just ecstatic about her new baby boy. I'm sure my father was so caught up with making a living that he didn't notice something was different with this birth.

Two weeks after leaving the hospital Mark became very sick.

My mother was frantic as she described Mark's high fever and convulsions over the phone to the doctor, who ordered her to come directly to the hospital with Mark and my father.

After examining my brother, the doctor said, "Your son has pneumonia, severe diarrhea, and he has a heart murmur. Your son also has Down syndrome. I'm sure you noticed the slanted eyes, one of the symptoms."

Why didn't he sit down and thoroughly explain this condition? Instead he paused, allowing time for the Mack Truck announcement to sink in.

"You can leave him in the hospital or you can let him stay at home. I-I-I don't know if he will live," he continued.

Sternly and confidently, my mother replied, "I want to do everything I can to save my baby."

Because the doctor knew that Mark had Down syndrome, did he secretly feel that this little baby would be a burden and better off dead? The doctor told my parents he waited so long to deliver the bad news because he didn't want my mother to be alone.

A diagnosis of this magnitude needs to be made in front of both parents.

Mark made it through that critical evening. After that crisis the doctor said, "I suggest you put this baby in an institution. He will never walk nor will he ever talk. He most likely will not live to see his sixth birthday."

My father's pride triggered the immediate response, "You know, doctor, we will NOT put our child in an institution and you know, one day, HE'LL be a doctor!"

That first year, however, was not easy. Mark was in the hospital more than he was out. There were numerous complications including double pneumonia. Mark had to have an expensive special type of powdered milk. The bills kept coming, and my parents couldn't handle all of the escalating costs.

Dad especially was concerned about his ability to pay. He knew there was one sure way his family could handle the never-ending health care Mark would need; he enlisted in the United States Army where the family's health needs would be included in the benefits of his service to our country. Although my father enrolled to secure his family's stability, he came to love his new career and served with honor for more than twenty-five years.

My father has since shared that he has felt guilty about Mark. Before joining the Army, Dad owned a sign painting business. Networking with clients after hours at a local tavern, he frequently left my pregnant mother alone with three other little ones. Worrying that God gave him this child as a punishment, he confided that although it had been difficult, Mark became a blessing.

"I don't think God works like that, Dad," I told him one day. "You see, you chose to keep and take care of Mark, treating him just like your other children, which helped him to walk, talk, swim, and do many things that an institution might not have accomplished. Ultimately, you gave him love, which allowed him to flourish. Maybe God chose you and mom because he knew that Mark would have the devotion of his brothers and sisters and he would be nurtured with care. You were not given this child out of punishment, but out of knowing that our family would be better for having known and worked with a child with Down syndrome."

Growing up in a large military family in which money was ALWAYS a concern, love for Mark was not. My sister, Dianna, and I being the oldest siblings (three and four years older than Mark) helped care for our five younger brothers. We treated Mark as an equal to his brothers—he was just one more added to a multitude of lively, mischievous youngsters!

Perhaps it was low muscle tone (one of the symptoms of Down syndrome) that delayed Mark's ability to walk until he was four years old. My mother damaged her back toting him around on her hip. She would sling the hefty guy to her side, which threw a disc in her backbone out of place. The day he took his first steps was quite celebratory, especially because the physician who suggested institutionalization had said he would never walk.

While my sister and I were constant companions growing up so close in age, my brother Steve had a different relationship with his closest male sibling who was only two years younger. He has enlightened us with stories of how he would get into fights defending Mark when children poked fun at him. We had neighbors who wouldn't let their children play with Mark because they feared THEIR children might catch my brother's "disease." In our family, however, Mark was accepted and loved unconditionally.

When I look at the lives that Mark has touched, it amazes me. My own daughter now has a master's degree in special education and teaches students with special needs. My niece Megan is certified to help children with autism. Jacqueline, another niece, is working toward a degree in occupational therapy so that she can work one-on-one with the disabled. Careers that might not have been considered were cultivated through their experiences with Uncle Mark.

We have progressed light years in knowledge about Down syndrome. Research has given babies born today with this condition a much brighter future. From the life expectancy of nine years old in 1920 to a life expectancy of over fifty today, it is obvious that much has been learned and research still continues.

While there are guidelines regarding physical and cognitive development, it is impossible to predict the future of a child with Down syndrome – just as it is for any other child. No professional can look at a child and tell you how intelligent, successful or independent he or she will be in 20, 30, or 50 years.

"A Promising Future Together," National Down Syndrome Society, accessed online at www.udss.org, 1/17/2004. Reprinted with permission from NDSS

"Right after every birth Ruth looked lovely, but I will never forget the day Mark was born. While lying in bed that April morning, her face had a beautiful color and she looked so happy. She was glowing like a light and reminded me of an angel."

Carroll Simpson

Part I

My Brother's Adult Years Begin
Life in Rural Virginia

Between the years 1990 and 2010, the number of persons with Down's syndrome over the age of 40 years is expected to increase by 75%, but the number with Down's syndrome over 50 years will rise by 200% (Steffalaar and Evenhuis 1989)

V.P. Prasher, MD, "Longevity and Down's syndrome," Medical Library, The Down's Syndrome Medical Interest Group (DSMIG).
Accessed online at www.dsmig.org on January 28, 2005.
Reprinted with permission

Hi! I'm Mark Simpson

One extra chromosome... that one extra chromosome made all the difference. That one extra chromosome had such power to produce a condition that would affect my brother's brain, his physical features, his speech, his life. Down syndrome was a condition foreign to my family until Mark was born. In 1952 not much was understood by anyone about the disorder. From a life expectancy of nine years in 1920 to a life expectancy of over fifty today, it is obvious that much has been learned. Research still continues.

When my father retired from the service in 1969, he bought his parent's home in Sycamore, Virginia, just outside the little town of Gretna where Dad grew up. The modest municipality of Gretna is a lazy southern town where I always delight in being greeted at the city limits by a huge billboard that reads "WELCOME TO GRETNA, AIN'T NO BIG THING BUT WE'RE GROWING."

While his younger years were spent on several different Army posts, much of Mark's adult life was spent on my parent's farm. My parents' fifty-seven acres of rolling hills are picturesque, with the farm nestled in the middle. Despite the red clay Piedmont soil, each summer my mother's fertilized garden reaps delicious produce. With the farm providing an abundance of simple chores, including weeding the garden, feeding the animals, and getting up hay, my brother was happy and fulfilled there for many years.

On the farm, Mark had genuine responsibilities with a few adjustments for his special needs. As he mastered simple household chores and outside duties, my brother became quite a farmhand. Mark helped get up hay, took out the trash, loaded the dishwasher, swept floors, weeded the garden, shoveled snow, fed animals, and willingly, although very slowly, persevered to help wherever he was needed.

He always admired my father, trying to emulate his every move. Mark was eager to work along side his dad on the never-ending chores. Once he was moving a load of fence posts in a wheelbarrow to the pasture where Dad was building a fence. As the obstinate apparatus kept falling over, out would tumble his heavy load. One by one Mark would place the posts back into the wheelbarrow and started moving again. Plop! Over his load would turn once more.

Disgusted but undaunted, he would return the posts into the wheelbarrow. Neither wavering nor discouraged, he kept to the task until it was done, although it took hours as his load kept toppling over.

Another time Dad was building a fire in the wood stove, which was housed in the basement. He wanted to empty ashes out of the stove into an old metal coal bucket.

"Go get the coal bucket, Mark," Dad called. Mark came but he had retrieved a five, gallon container—not the coal bucket.

"Mark, I told you to bring me the COAL bucket. This is not it."

Again my brother went outside and came back with yet another container, but not the right one.

"Mark, this is not right, I want the COAL bucket," my father reiterated.

Mark was exasperated, "It is COLD!"

Dad immediately realized there was a miscommunication and Mark was bringing what he thought his father wanted: a COLD bucket!

Dad tried raising cattle after he retired, but when beef prices took a plunge, another opportunity came. He decided to restore a recreation center near the city of Alta Vista, not far from our home. My parents worked relentlessly to renovate an old run down pool and fishing area which they named Simpson's Recreation Center. It became a favorite summer relaxing reprieve for area residents. For seventeen years my folks owned the recreation center. My brother thrived there. He could fish and swim and have fun being around the daily vacationers. Mark loves people, and at the pool there was always something going on. He was never bored.

Reaching a height of five feet seven at maturity, Mark had the typical Down syndrome features including a thick neck, short stubby fingers, somewhat flat face, and slightly slanted eyes. Sprinkled across his nose were freckles that helped to brighten his face along with a wide playful, impish grin. Mark had been labeled "trainable" meaning he would never read nor write, but could be "trained" to perform simple tasks.

What made my brother "special" to our family was his personality. He had just enough mischief to be both irritating and endearing. Mark also displayed a stubborn streak. If he did not want to do something, only my father's voice or my sister could change his mind.

Mark was never devious nor vindictive. There wasn't a mean bone in his body. My brother was certainly stubborn and could become angry if he did not get his way, but he loved unconditionally. After stewing about a situation, he eventually came to the person he'd upset, said "I'm sorry" or "I 'pologize," and offered a huge hug of forgiveness.

Although he was certainly "equipped" to be sexually active (males with Down syndrome are believed to be impotent), we were relieved that Mark never acted on this. The purity mixed with his gregarious character made Mark a lovable and memorable soul.

Mark loved to sing. He would take his toy guitar out in front of the old chicken coop, serenading the entire countryside. This became his concert hall, his stadium with sold out seats to the frogs, dogs, deer, fish, geese, cats, and other wildlife. On the hill across from the farm, the wailing strains of his unintelligible, unmelodious singing were still audible. His only applause was an occasional honk from a goose or yelp from a dog.

Far from being shy, my brother was an open, friendly sort of guy. When he traveled into town with my parents, as if running for public office, Mark reached out to unsuspecting strangers. Grasping each hand with a firm handshake, he said, "Hi, I'm Mark Simpson."

Folks in the small town came to know and accept my brother. Mr. Adams at the corner grocery store would always give Mark change from a $10 bill in singles, knowing that Mark thought 10 ones were worth more than 2 fives. Quantity got his attention!

Even after Mark left to live in a group home, he continued to have that sparkle in his eye, coming up to greet anyone who visited with, "Hi, I'm Mark Simpson."

The childhood experience of families with older sons and daughters was often very different from that experienced by families now. In the past, based on information provided by healthcare and education professionals, families often had very low expectations for their son or daughter. Good health care was often unavailable to children with Down syndrome. School, social, recreational, and work opportunities were often limited or nonexistent. We now know that early intervention is very beneficial for children with Down syndrome (Anderson et al., 2003; Guralnick, 1998).

Dennis McGuire, Ph.D and Brian Chicoine, M.D.,
Mental Wellness in Adults with Down Syndrome
(Bethesda, MD: Woodbine House, Inc., 2006)
Reprinted with permission

Mark after swim practice for the Special Olympics.

Mark with his mother. They had a very special bond.

The Adult Down Syndrome Center has discovered that one of the most interesting and consistent findings for people with Down syndrome is the need for sameness, repetition and order in their lives. They call this tendency the "groove" because thoughts and actions of people tend to follow well worn paths, or grooves.

Dennis McGuire, PhD, "The Groove," Adult Down Syndrome Center Newsletter, Spring 1999. Accessed online at www.advocatehealth.com/adultdown/publications.html, May 20, 2003.
Reprinted with permission

Call The Sheriff

"Call the Sheriff."
"I'm gonna call the Sheriff."
"Call the Sheriff!"
He was in his twenties when I first recall Mark's repetitions. The phrase "Call the Sheriff" was repeated numerous times. There might be a break of ten minutes or even half a day, but the familiar phrase always returned. Mark did not seem to realize that he was repeating. Although he gave the impression that he could control the repetitions, if you told Mark not to say something one more time, in less than three minutes, you would hear him whisper it again. It was hopeless.

I think the phrase came from my father, who might have been mad at some occurrence at our family operated pool or a political quibble in town and had said, "I'm going to call the sheriff." Most likely, this comment was uttered in the heat of a discussion, but somehow it stuck with Mark. Every time he would get rattled about anything, he would say, "Call the sheriff."

If someone left a piece of trash lying at the pool he would wail, "Call the sheriff."

If he got in trouble, he would proclaim loudly "Call the sheriff!".

When the least irritation came into his day, Mark would declare "Call the sheriff." To say the least, it drained energy from everyone around him. After months of hearing this phrase repeated ceaselessly, my parents' patience wore thin.

One day, Mom and Dad decided to see if actually "calling the sheriff" would stop the incessant repetition. After one particularly draining day, Mom called an acquaintance who worked as a policeman asking if he might come over and meet Mark. Perhaps seeing the real sheriff might be a cure.

The officer drove out to the farm and rang the doorbell. Mark sauntered to the door to greet whomever the dogs were making such a fuss about. There standing at the door was a policeman dressed smartly in his blue uniform with a badge and a wide-brimmed hat. The sight must have startled Mark as he stepped back in shock.

"Mark, I understand you called the sheriff," the officer said in a gruff voice.

Mark, too stunned to speak, said nothing.

"You know, Mark, calling the sheriff is a serious matter. You can't just call the sheriff for any little thing. We're very busy on important crimes. Now what is your problem?" continued the officer.

No response.

"I'm sure you're a good boy. You just pay attention and listen to your parents. You can only call the sheriff for serious crimes, ok?" he said as he smiled and shook Mark's hand.

The family walked the officer outside to his car where Mark became even more impressed when he saw the police officer's car. As he noted the red light on top, he recognized this was truly an important officer of the law, the REAL sheriff.

As the "sheriff" drove out of the driveway, Mark stood and stared until the squad car was out of sight.

Shortly after that meeting, the "call the sheriff" repetitions began to wane and eventually ceased altogether, only to be replaced by other endless phrases Mark would find interesting. Every family member can share a favorite Mark repetition, such as "baseball bat," "California, California," or "don't call me hard-headed." He would love to get in your face and echo his favorite word or phrase of the moment.

The phrases were like old records that would get stuck, catch, and repeat: "Call the sheriff" began an eternity of vocal repetitions that became part of Mark's personality which we all just learned to endure.

Although there are many benefits and advantages, there are also some disadvantages to grooves that sometimes cause problems. Some of the problems need not be serious if handled appropriately by caregivers. For example a person may be interested in a particular issue, such as a favorite sports team, which they retell over and over to family and friends While this may be a minor irritant to caregivers, it is not necessarily a problem that interferes with important spheres of living. Additionally there are grooves that may be adaptive if done at the appropriate time or place.

Dennis McGuire, PhD, "The Groove," Adult Down Syndrome Center Newsletter, Spring 1999. Accessed online at www.advocatehealth.com/adultdown/publications.html, May 20, 2003.
Reprinted with permission

Mark loved summers at the Simpson recreation center, especially the pool!

Over time, parents learn that there is no time schedule that governs the pace at which their child with Down syndrome learns new skills. Provided that the child is in good health and is provided with opportunities to grow and learn, development will continue throughout the individual's lifetime.

Dorothy Robison, Marty Wyngaarden Krauss, Marsha Mailick Seltzer, "Does Parenting Ever End?," National Down Syndrome Society. Accessed online at www.ndss.org, May 19, 2003. Reprinted with permission

I Can Do That

"Oh, my God, he's drowned!"

My mother had panicked. To her it seemed like it was more than ten minutes ago when Mark had plunged into the pool, diving under water.

Mark had an intense desire to learn to swim. This longing was spurred on while working at Simpson's Recreation Center, my parent's seasonal business. The center included two ponds for fishing, a go-cart track, a one-acre pool where my father had painted cartoon characters at the bottom, a diving board, a steep slide that landed one into the water, a sandy beach around the entire pool, plus a delicious snack bar. It was a great summer relaxation area for local families and a terrific playground for Mark.

Mark vigilantly watched his brother Ken teach swimming each day as he played in the shallow end of the pool. His desire to cross the threshold into the deep end to enjoy the water slide and swim like his brothers and the big kids grew daily.

One day, Mark pointed to the deep end of the pool at one of my brothers swimming and said, "I can do that."

"You mean you THINK you can swim?" Ken questioned Mark. He was sure my brother just THOUGHT he could swim.

Mark shook his head and repeated, "I can do that." Ken agreed to let him try and took him to the diving board. Mark eagerly walked to the deep end of the pool. He looked out at my brother, then looked at the water, and back at my brother again. Ken shook his head saying, "You can do it."

A massive swinging of his arms began to give him momentum; after about the third swing he was propelled into the pool. Instead of staying on top, however, he began swimming under water! My father nearby was watching cautiously along with Ken.

Because the pool was extraordinarily large, Mark seemed to disappear. My father tried to be patient as he felt his heart sink; it had been at least three minutes and my brother was nowhere to be seen.

"He's still not up, Dad!" even my brother was getting concerned. Ken realized that Mark had been watching him teach lessons, but didn't think he could truly swim. Mark had been under too long.

When mom realized what transpired, she demanded, "Carroll, send Ken in to get him!" She was in full panic mode.

Dad nodded for my brother to jump in to rescue our beloved Mark from the bottom of the pool.

But just as suddenly as he had disappeared, Mark emerged from the water with a huge splash, his face red from holding his breath for so long. He had swum the entire length of the pool!

Spying us, he smiled and was ready to do it again!

We were relieved—and shocked. Not only could Mark swim, but he had great breath control!

Mark's observation skills could be keen when he desired something. As a swimmer, he had more endurance and became the most adept of my five brothers. After this experience, he was allowed in the deep end, and his swimming skills improved enormously. He could swim for hours. He had permission to swim only when someone was there to watch him, as my mother didn't trust Mark to be alone.

Watching my brother swim was a delight. He simply loved to jump off the board. He had his own style which would never garner a medal, but was amusing to observe. After several attempts of swinging his arms, he would catapult himself off the diving board. As he jumped, his tongue would stick out as if somehow it helped him soar through the air into the water. Mark swam back and forth across the mammoth pool, rested at one side for a few moments and repeated the pattern. He never tired of this "lap" swimming and did so for hours until my father made him vacate the pool.

Swimming could get Mark in trouble. He never wanted to come out of the water. On Mark's visits to my home later in his life, we had never ending pool problems. I had to bribe him to get out of the water, telling him that when he saw me, he must come to the edge of the pool and get out. If he did, I would get him coffee (a favorite drink) on the way home. He played a game with me. It went something like this: He saw me as I entered the pool area. Pretending NOT to see me, he promptly swam in the opposite direction. Glancing at me, he realized we had made eye contact. Knowing at that moment he had to come, in S-L-O-W m-o-t-i-o-n this water fanatic would take one…more…lap before coming to the edge of the pool.

After he moved to a group home, he still loved to swim. The activity one afternoon was to go for a dip in a nearby pool. After an adequate time in the water (never enough for Mark), he was told to get out. Reluctantly he obliged and began changing his clothes, but he kept eyeing the pool. The temptation became too much. Before the staff could get to him, off came the belt, off came the pants, and into the pool he jumped, white underwear and all! Mark soon understood that he could not swim in a public place in his underwear. It was some time before he was allowed to return to that pool!

Mark's sport of choice with Special Olympics became swimming. We visited one year so we could attend the swimming competition. If you ever want to have some-thing pull at your heartstrings, attend or volunteer at the Special Olympics. That day I'll never forget. These special competitors take this seriously and love the attention. This non-profit association is very well organized with each Olympian having a sponsor. My brother loved his sponsor and his time competing at the yearly event.

I will never forget watching Mark receive his medals, ceremoniously standing on a platform holding his arms up in celebration proudly displaying his medals which he would not take off. He even wore them to church!

MARK SIMPSON has overcome his handicap and learned to swim.

There are a number of skills such as driving and hunting which Mark was not allowed to pursue, but with swimming, when he said, "I can do that", he was right!

Don't lower your expectations because your baby has Down syndrome. You will never know what your child is capable of if you don't give him or her the chance to succeed. Today, individuals with Down syndrome are achieving more than we ever thought possible – due in part to higher expectations and more opportunities.

"A Promising Future Together,"
National Down Syndrome Society, accessed online at
www.ndss.org, May 19, 2003
Reprinted with permission

Children with Down syndrome have a wide range of abilities and talents, and each child develops at his or her own particular pace.

National Institue of Child Health & Human Development, "Facts About Down Syndrome", accessed online at www.nichd.nih.gov/publications/pubs/downsydrome/down.htm on January 3, 2004.

All That Crap

Everyone in the family has stories about Mark that we affectionately share. My sister Dianna's pet story reveals how my brother could solve problems.

Our family of seven children created vast quantities of laundry, including a hefty amount of ironing. When the ironing bag bulged, my sister and I knew that one of us would be commissioned to tackle the daunting hours of irksome pressing.

One day Dianna was ironing and needed hangers.

"Mark," she called, "I need hangers!" She held up an example and asked him to bring her some more. Upon his return, she noticed his hands were empty.

"Mark, where are the hangers?"

"Nnnnooo hangers," he responded.

"Look, Mark, I need hangers. Go and get them. I don't care where you get them, but I need hangers now!"

Dianna watched as Mark walked away disgusted, mumbling and grumbling, "All that crap." Whenever he was frustrated with us or his environment, "All that crap" was a common mantra. That winter my brother had crooned this tune quite often. No doubt the phrase came from something my brothers had brought home from school.

Mark disappeared and much to my sister's delight came back shortly with fifteen hangers.

"Wow, great Mark! Good boy," she commended his efforts.

An hour or two later, Dianna was hanging the freshly pressed clothing on a closet rack. She spied piles of something that looked like folded garments on the floor of the closet.

"Someone forgot to put their clothes in the drawer," she thought as she bent down to check out the stacks. Then she had a revelation. The clothing she discovered should have been hanging in the closet ON HANGERS, not on the floor! Immediately she knew that Mark had taken perfectly ironed items off their hangers. Voila, that's where he "found" the fifteen hangers! Knowing that he would be trouble for this, he had carefully folded and neatly stacked the clothing on the floor. I'm sure he was hoping no one would notice the new pile!

Mark had taken a lemon and made lemonade; he was ordered to get hangers, and so he did. He disposed of "all that crap" by solving a problem HIS way!

Dianna smiled to herself and never let Mark know that she had found the folded clothing. She wondered if she would have been as clever and inventive as her brother when faced with a similar challenge.

Self-determination is related to motivation...true self-determination is demonstrated when a person makes choices based on what he knows and believes, not on what he has been told to do, or is expected to do.

From Jan Blacher,"Self-Determination: Why Is It Important for Your Child?" April 7, 2004, National Down Syndrome Society. Accessed online at www.ndss.org on July 12, 2004. Reprinted with permission

Self-determination skills can be encouraged by increasing interest, enjoyment and satisfaction in home and school activities in several ways. For example: Teach the child to value and understand an assigned activity......Give the child opportunities to try new things and take risks.

From Jan Blacher, "Self-Determination: Why is it important for Your Child?" April 7, 2004, National Down Syndrome Society. Accessed online at www.ndss.org on July 12, 2004. Reprinted with permission

I 'member That

Mark plunged into a job with such zest that at times he went too far. He loved any physical activity and worked diligently, immersing himself into any task almost to the point of overdoing it.

When he was fifteen and in a special education class, he was once given the job of "straightening the room." Some administrators were coming to tour the school, and the faculty was working hard to prepare. As the time for the visit approached, Mark's teacher left the room to run an errand.

As she hurried back to the classroom, the educator was aghast at what she discovered outside the door. In his enthusiasm to clean up, Mark had decided to do a deep cleaning. He had moved each and every desk into the hall! What could his teacher say? She had given him instructions, but Mark had perceived them differently. She could not remain angry at someone with such an innocent motive.

Just as the special ed teacher had to scramble with the consequences of leaving Mark on his own to interpret vague instructions, my parents often faced trouble in the Simpson household with a capital "M" for Mark. They learned a valuable lesson for living with an adult with Down syndrome: instructions need to be extremely specific and focused. And for goodness sake, check on the progress frequently to be sure instructions were followed as intended!

Such was the case on a sunny morning when my parents decided to continue building a new fence. Since my brother was physically a strong man, he would be of help. Working outside and at the pool, he had acquired a great tan and physique. He loved re-ceiving compliments on his fine muscle tone, finding every opportunity to display his prowess. Holding his arm up in a muscle-man pose and picking up a heavy item, he could confirm his strength and attract accolades.

Mom and Dad thought they could trust Mark to use the post hole digger, a relatively heavy hand tool with two handles. At the end of the handles are two shovels bolted together, allowing the apparatus to bore holes in the soil. After cutting into the earth, Mark could sepa-rate the handles as the shovels gathered the dirt. With many repetitions, a deep but narrow hole (about eight inches in diameter) for each fence post could be hollowed out. My father knew Mark would have the strength to handle the job.

Dad demonstrated the motions with the digger twice. "I 'member that," Mark addressed my Dad as if he truly understood his instructions. My parents left Mark as they went to another part of the farm to work.

They must have forgotten to check on him. When they returned, their muscle-man had dug such a deep hole for the fence post that the hole was deeper than the post!

"Mark, you sure have dug some hole here!" Dad reacted with shock.

Then they helped my ambitious brother refill the hole with dirt until the post was the proper height. My parents laughed, knowing they had left Mark alone for too long.

He clearly knew how to operate the post hole digger; he just became ambitious and didn't realize when he should quit.

You could not give Mark a job without constant vigilance or you would have to accept the consequences. Whatever his mind's eye saw was quite often not in snyc with yours! His "I 'member that" might not have matched what you remembered!

Findings from several studies indicated that IQ levels among students and adults with cognitive and learning disabilities did not make a difference in their ability to learn and use self-determination skills. This important finding should encourage parents and teachers to have high expectations, and a belief that all students can benefit from learning self-determination skills, regardless of their cognitive ability.

From Jan Blacher, "Self-Determination: Why is it important for Your Child?" April 7, 2004, National Down Syndrome Society. Accessed online at www.ndss.org on July 12, 2004. Reprinted with permission

Mark lounging in the pool, waving.

The most common (groove) centers on personal preferences for such things as music, sports teams, or celebrities. Grooves may also include such personal issues as a favorite relative or a love interest. Also common are grooves which have independence issues as a theme. These are often expressed as "I want to do it (a particular activity) by myself and in my own way".

Dennis McGuire, PhD, "The Groove," Adult Down Syndrome Newsletter, Spring 1999. Accessed online at www.advocatehealth.com/adultdown/publications.html, May 20, 2003
Reprinted with permission

I Want Sunshine

All of us have idiosyncrasies of some type—behaviors that are distinctive and sometimes irritating. People with average or higher intelligence levels usually control when and where idiosyncratic behaviors are displayed, but people with Down syndrome are not usually aware or concerned that a behavior might be distracting.

So, it was with Mark's obsession with the sun. I don't know how this began, but Mark loved sunshine and anything that symbolized the sun. Dad might have made some comment about wanting to see sunshine during a rainy period, and Mark picked up on it.

Mark would look for anything with sun. A yellow ball with a smiley face was popular at the time and Mark loved that image, thus emerged another connection with the sun. People even gave him smiley T-shirts that he wore until they became tattered, falling to pieces!

Then out of the blue in the 1990s, my brother began to focus on the MasterCard™ image—it looked like a sunrise to Mark. Every time he saw a MasterCard symbol, he would walk over, bend down, and repeatedly point to it. Do you have any idea how many businesses display that symbol prominently? I was amazed that every time we were with Mark, he seemed to find that symbol.

My nephew Daniel described a time when he was walking with Mark at a mall. Daniel glanced away, and suddenly Mark had disappeared! My nephew frantically looked around and finally found him outside a store pointing to the MasterCard symbol. "Sunshine!" he exclaimed, turning around grinning.

My brother Steve was traveling with Mark once and stopped to get gas.

"Mark, stay in the car, I'm going in to pay," Steve explained. He came out a few minutes later, but there was no Mark. A surge of panic struck Steve as he immediately began searching. He double-checked inside the car, the pumps, the surrounding grassy areas, and even the bathrooms. He glanced back at the building where he had just paid for gas. There was Mark, bent over in front of the gas station window, his nose almost touching the glass, pointing to the Master Card symbol, "I see sunshine," he smiled.

My husband, Clark, gave Mark his own expired MasterCard, which he kept in his wallet to show everyone. I'm happy he has never had access to using that "sunshine" card as he loved to shop. Mark never missed a chance to point out the MasterCard icon—his sunshine. It was awkward when my brother suddenly and incessantly pointed to MasterCard logos in public. People tended to stare and seemed to wonder, "Is that guy some kind of a nut?" I really could not stop to explain that my brother was obsessed with MasterCard™ signs. I simply tried to ignore them and focused on Mark.

What a metaphor! Mark was actually sunshine to us——well, sunshine with a chance of clouds!

The groove is a powerful means of expression and communication. This is especially true for people with Down syndrome, who have limited ability to express themselves verbally. Each groove is a clear and unambiguous statement of a personal choice or preference.

Dennis McGuire, PhD, "The Groove," Adult Down Syndrome Center Newsletter, Spring 1999. Accessed online at www.advocatehealth.com/adultdown/publications.html, May 20, 2003
Reprinted with permission

Mark proudly displaying his fake "sunshine" tatoo.

Mark shows off his muscles while holding his nephew.

A groove (actions of people tending to follow fairly well worn paths) may become a maladaptive rut when it interferes with functioning in the important spheres of living...Some persons may make poor decisions, which then become "bad habits".

Dennis McGuire, PhD., "The Groove", Adult Down Syndrome Center Newsletter, Spring 1999. Accessed online at www.advocatehealth.com/adultdown/publications.html, May 20, 2003. Reprinted with permission

I DID NOT! I Didn't Do It!

"Mark, look at your pants, what is that on your pants? That is spit!" I was livid that Mark had such a disgusting habit.

"I DID NOT DO IT!" he loudly proclaimed.

Mark's immaturity made him resistant to admitting lies or other misdeeds. He knew the consequences, and he wanted no part of a punishment. So he lied instead. Unlike a normal older child, however, Mark would not retreat. He tried to conceal his mistakes, which made it difficult to handle his numerous habits. Some quirks were accepted and merely ignored at home, but in the outside world some of Mark's behaviors were downright embarrassing.

One particularly troublesome behavior was spitting. We siblings believed this started innocently enough. Mark tried to emulate those around him. Although he struggled with Dad as the family disciplinarian, Mark truly loved him and imitated his behavior. For example, each morning Mark sat down, had coffee, opened the newspaper, turning pages intensely and staring at the print, just like a sophisticated stock broker mulling over the stock news in the financial section. A stranger would think that he was actually reading, but with closer scrutiny he would find that the paper was upside down! Although Mark recognized the McDonald's arches, the Cracker Barrel sign, and his name, he could not read.

Unfortunately, perusing the newspaper was not the only habit of Dad's that Mark emulated. When Dad would spit, Mark would spit. Of course, Dad did so discreetly and infrequently and only outside on his farm. Mark copied this up to a point, but with exaggeration and without discretion. Mark would make loud guttural sounds, pull out his handkerchief, and spit into it with gusto. If he lost his handkerchief, he used his hands and wiped them on his clothes. We all chastised Mark whenever we caught him:

"Mark, did you SPIT that on your hands?"

"I did not!"

"Yes, you did! Mark, that is gross."

"I did not, I did not do it."

It became a vicious cycle. Exasperated, one of us simply said, "Mark, we are not going to hug you or touch you if you do that again. Use your handkerchief."

His behavior improved somewhat, but Mark continued to struggle with controlling this unhygienic bad habit.

Attempts to directly force the person having difficulty with a groove will usually worsen the problem. Caregivers who are most successful at helping in these circumstances, understand the need and benefits of grooves. Instead of a direct and forceful approach, they will slowly and gently help the person resolve the issue in a positive way.

Dennis McGuire, PhD., "The Groove", Adult Down Syndrome Newsletter, Spring 1999. Accessed online at www.advocatehealth.com/adultdown/publications.html, May 20, 2003.
Reprinted with permission

In order for individuals with Down syndrome to build self-confidence, it is of paramount importance that they not be viewed as helpless. They should be encouraged to become as independent as possible, take responsibility for self-care, and develop a certain degree of autonomy. When young people with Down syndrome are helped to build on their demonstrated competencies and proven strengths, they are able to experience success, which in turn, enhances their self-esteem."

Siegfried M. Pueschel, *Young People with Down Syndrome: Transition from Childhood to Adulthood* (National Down Syndrome Society, 2001 Compendium). Accessed online at www.ndss.org, on January 15, 2004.
Reprinted with permission

I Appreciate That

Sometimes we forgot. We forgot that Mark wanted the rites of passage that his siblings had experienced. We had all earned our driver's licenses, dated, gone to proms, graduated from high school, and left the nest. I recall when Mark snuck the car keys so he could drive and promptly rammed the car into a tree! We became caught up in our own milestones, not appreciating that Mark might enjoy celebrating his own personal successes, other than just his birthday.

Perhaps that is why my sister and I decided in 1979 that Mark needed a graduation ceremony. Public Law 94-142 (legislation authorizing free public education to all handicapped children between the ages of three and twenty-one) was not adopted until 1975, when Mark was twenty-three. Precluded from experiencing the benefits of this critical piece of educational ruling, his only exposure to school was attending a few special education programs in the 1960s.

Knowing that he would not have an opportunity to celebrate this benchmark and knowing how much he loved attention and parties—my sister and I decided that a graduation for Mark was in order. The first dilemma was determining from WHERE and for WHAT our brother would graduate. After brainstorming with Dad, we realized that Mark actually knew quite a bit about farming. That was it! Mark could take an oral examination and graduate from the Simpson Farm School. We explained to Mark that this was a test and if he passed he would graduate like his brothers and sisters.

"What do you think of that, Mark?" I inquired looking into his eyes for understanding. His face brightened. "Do you think you know about farming?" I asked.

He nodded, "Yep."

We sat around the kitchen table as my father grilled Mark on all aspects of farming. He asked how to get in the wood, check the cows, take out the trash, weed the garden, feed the dogs, mend fences, and help get up hay. In most cases, Mark would pantomime his answers, because long vocal responses were usually unintelligible to us.

With each answer, Dad nodded and said, "That's correct, Son." He recorded the answers on a pad of paper, confirming the serious nature of the matter.

Occasionally my father had to prod his candidate to elicit the acceptable answer, but at the end of the exam (which lasted about fifteen minutes), Dad announced: "You passed the farm school test, Mark. Congratulations!"

I'm not quite sure Mark understood exactly what he had just accomplished, but since we were all clapping and hugging him, he knew this had to be a good thing.

Our second dilemma was deciding who should be invited to the ceremony. We wanted the guests to treat the occasion as a "true" graduation and celebration. After reviewing a guest list that included only those who knew Mark well, we decided not to worry and began inviting a number of my parents' friends and relatives to the Saturday event. With family alone, there would be a full audience. We would show our congratulatory spirit and figured friends and neighbors would follow our lead.

Saturday came with a bright sun, one that matched Mark's spirits. He was excited! Since this graduation was just for him, we wanted to make sure Mark stood out with the proper commencement attire. Somewhere in her voluminous costume closet mother located a cap and gown—it was amazing what that woman had stashed in every nook and cranny of her home!

Whether it was curiosity or simply a desire to support our grad, many friends and relatives came. The beauty of the ceremony was its respectful tone. No one prompted the guests to be serious, nor did we tell everyone to have fun and make Mark "feel good." The truth is all of the invited guests responded as if this were an authentic graduation. It could have been a celebration of Mark finishing Harvard. People dressed and acted as if this occasion was of utmost importance, and to Mark, it was indeed.

My husband, Clark, played "Pomp and Circumstance" in the organ mode of his portable piano, as the dignitaries paraded into the house from the outside. My father, as President of the Simpson Farm School, led the procession followed by our local parish priest. Mark stood in his graduation regalia as proudly as if he were being presented with the Medal of Honor.

After a prayer by our priest and a brief speech by my father, Mark's name was called and he was presented with his diploma. As he stood there sporting the ceremonial garb, the mortarboard's tassel tickling his face, tears began to well up in his eyes. He was proud, he was touched, and he was graduating! After Mark accepted the rolled up certificate tied neatly with a ribbon hastily taken from Mom's gift closet, we all applauded.

Mark looked up at my father, "I appreciate that," he said through his tears.

Wanting to keep the formal event moving, Clark immediately began to play the recessional so that the ensemble could parade back out the door.

After the ceremony came the real reason Mark remembered all of us and our graduations— the presents! Oh, was he excited! Mark loves money, T-shirts, hats, and food. I don't remember everything he received that day; in fact, I hardly remember the party afterwards. I do know that I will never forget the image of Mark in tears, so happy to be graduating, so happy to be treated just like his brothers and sisters. It took little effort, but it made a big impact on those attending and most especially to a young man whom God had blessed to bring into our lives.

It is too often assumed that young people with disabilities have few, if any, strengths or gifts. Uncovering, acknowledging, and letting others know the personal capacities of your teen/young adults not only have the potential to begin changing attitudes of peers, but increases the likelihood that your young person will experience belonging and valuing in the community.

Brian Abery, "Ways to Enhance Social Inclusion," Down Syndrome News, Vol. 29, #4, newsletter of the National Down Syndrome Congress, 1370 Center Drive, Suite 102, Atlanta, Georgia 30338, www.ndsccenter.org.
Reprinted with permission

Historically, employment in the competitive labor force for individuals with disabilities, including people with Down syndrome, was viewed as unattainable. If individuals with disabilities received vocational training or employment services, they most likely received them in sheltered (segregated) environments.

Darlene D. Unger, "Working in the Community through Supported Employment", National Down Syndrome Society. Accessed online at www.ndss.org on August 30, 2004.
Reprinted with permission

Gimme a Job

"Mom, why is Mark sitting out front in the cold with his lunch box? Does he realize it is Christmas Eve?" I asked when we arrived at my parents' home for the holidays in 1998.

"He doesn't quite understand that the sheltered workshop is closed for the holidays," she explained. "He'll come back in eventually but right now you'll find him patiently sitting on the porch waiting for the bus to take him to work."

While Mark was situated outside he would occasionally check his watch (although he could not tell time), as if wondering why the bus was late. Mom had tried to explain the workshop was closed for the holidays, but Mark loved his job so much that he got angry. He still got dressed, grabbed his lunch box, and headed for the porch for several days until he accepted the fact that there would be no bus until vacation was over.

According to Maslow's Hierarchy of Needs, after the necessities of food, clothing, and shelter have been met, people need to feel self-actualized. They need to feel valued. Mark was no different. A lower IQ does not involve a lower psychological need to live a satisfied, happy life. My parents had treated Mark like the rest of his siblings. He grew up doing the same household chores we had done. Completing tasks was fulfilling to him.

After all six of us "flew from the nest", Mark's responsibilities were measurably more important: bringing in the wood, stacking wood, picking up trash, loading the dishwasher, unloading the dishwasher, vacuuming, and getting the mail. These tasks were perfect for Mark: simple and repetitive. All were well-suited for a person with Down syndrome. When most of us whined, abhorring menial duties, Mark found work quite satisfying.

Dad always rewarded his son with an allowance at the end of each week. Payment was given all in one dollar bills because Mark was more impressed with the numbers of bills instead of the number on the bill.

Slowly and carefully each dollar bill was placed, one by one, in his wallet. He loved payday!

Although he enjoyed the farm, as his siblings started working in town and then moved away, Mark began yearning for a "real" job. When a sheltered workshop opened nearby, my parents were delighted. Mark would have an opportunity to meet more people and get out into the community. He would receive a small paycheck with a real job. He was excited!

For thirteen years my brother was happy and content working at the sheltered workshop. Again he had menial tasks, but he loved jobs like boxing nails or whatever was asked of him. Five days a week Mark would be transported from the farm to the workshop. The convenience of having the van come directly to the farm was a blessing. The workshop provided someone else to help Mom and Dad with supervision of their son, a well deserved respite. Mark was happy, my parents were happy.

Although most days went smoothly, there were times

when my brother misbehaved. Occasionally he would sneak snacks and drinks. The cognitive portion of his brain could neither add nor subtract but he could hide sodas and goodies that he wanted in the most innovative places. Even at home, we were amazed to find cans of soft drinks he had hidden in rafters and behind toilets. The workshop supervisor tried to understand Mark and work with my parents when an issue arose. Behavior modification was usually successful.

When management changed, however, trouble began. My guess is that the city could not find a person with special education qualifications. There are shortages in this occupation nationwide, and in small towns the problem is particularly acute. Mark did not like change, and the new workshop manager, from my parent's perspective, did not appear to understand how to handle people with Down syndrome.

The last straw came when Mark decided to leave the workshop in the middle of the day. For some unknown reason he became angry, marched out of the building and was found walking along the railroad tracks. Fearing perhaps litigation and loss of control, the manager promptly dismissed Mark.

I remember visiting home after his dismissal. The first words out of Mark's mouth were, "Gimme a job, gimme a job."

Case workers tried various placements—usually he lasted less than a month. Most employers did not understand how to deal with adults with special needs. If you were physically handicapped, the visible limitations were obvious; if you were mentally handicapped the limitations came out in odd behaviors that his supervisors were not equipped to handle.

Mark's final job lasted exactly one day. When the bus came at the end of the day to take Mark home, he did not want to leave. Being overly exuberant, he jumped to give his supervisor a giant hug. Mark might have thought a display of love for his job would permit him to stay. The employer, however, was not prepared and nearly fell over. Perhaps thinking he was being physically assaulted, this man could not deal with Mark and told his case worker that my brother could not return.

At age forty-eight, his classification with the state was now "high intensity," which meant he must have constant supervision. His "gimme a job" days were over.

One of the mechanisms through which individuals with Down syndrome may achieve successful, integrated employment outcome is through supported employment. Since supported employment emerged in federal legislation, the program has grown from 10,000 participants in 1986 to more than 140,000 in 1995. Characterized by individual support on and off the jobsite, initial and ongoing employment services, and assistance from a job coach, supported employment has become widely recognized as the most effective approach to achieving meaningful employment of individuals with a variety of disabilities.

Darlene D. Unger, "Working in the Community through Supported Employment", National Down Syndrome Society. Accessed online at www.ndss.org on August 30, 2004. Reprinted with permission

Mark enjoyed his years working at the sheltered workshop.

Part II

Am I My Brother's Keeper?
Siblings Share Mark's Care

Mark poses with his sisters just months before his death.

Mark strikes a silly pose at an amusement park when we took him on a Florida vacation.

Even when parents remain the primary caregivers, siblings tend to assume more responsibility for their brother or sister with a developmental disability as the parents and the individual age.

Gary B. Seltzer, "Sibling" the Next Generation of Family Supports?", IMPACT (Institute on Community Integration College of Education, University of Minnesota)
Volume 6, no. 1, pg. 16, Spring 1993.
Reprinted with permission

I Go With You

Mom needed a break. She rarely asked, so we knew she was serious when she did. By 1997 my parents had been Mark's caregivers for forty-five years and now that they were in their seventies, Mark was taking a toll on them. They were unwilling, however, to send him away. The images of dirty institutions where Mark would be tortured and drugged were somehow emblazoned on their minds. At that point, they would not even look at a "group home" because it was run by the "state."

All six of the siblings were willing to help, but there were barriers in each family, not the least of which was the spouses. Mark was classified as "high intensity." He had to be watched constantly, just like a five-year-old child. Adding him to a family unit created extra stress; some spouses he would obey, some he wouldn't. Unintentionally, Mark was an added burden.

At first we took turns housing my brother when my folks needed breaks. Since Dianna lived less than a quarter mile away, she "babysat" whenever they asked. At the same time Dianna became Mark's welcome escape from the daily routine at the farm. If there was a ball game, Dianna would pick up Mark and away they'd go. He was only too happy to tag along. She took him along with her family to the movies, roller skating, or dinner at a local restaurant. It was only natural that she became a favorite of his! As a teacher she had flexible summers, so she volunteered to watch Mark sporadically. The swimming pool in Dianna's backyard was a favorite of Mark's. She almost had to pry him out for meals.

My brother Steve and his wife Nancy drove Mark to their home in Hickory, North Carolina numerous times, keeping him for one-or-two week stays. Mark loved to go fishing with Steve and jogging with Nancy on her morning runs. When their daughters Megan and Jennifer were home, Mark loved the added commotion of the extra activity. He even began repeating the name of Megan's boyfriend, Hank, because of the kindness he displayed to my brother. Mark never wanted to leave as he enjoyed his North Carolina experiences so much.

Brothers Jeff and Ken were only a few years younger than Mark. Ken tells me that after Steve left home, they became Mark's protectors, always "standing up" for their brother, defending him when bullies tried to taunt him. The boys were very close to Mark, spending time with him while growing up on the farm and working at the recreation center. Ken even had Mark as a groomsman in his wedding.

After Jeff left home, Mark rarely saw him. His job as manager of an evening shift at a North Carolina company allowed little time for visits to the farm. Other than a few times when Jeff drove Mark to the group home after vacationing with the family, the two did not see each other.

Ken, on the other hand, had a more flexible schedule. He and his family lived on Smith Mountain Lake, less than forty-five minutes from Mom and Dad. Ken was a builder and Mark's strength actually was a help with simple tasks. Several times Mark would work at Ken's job site, cleaning up sawdust and the messes that occur during construction. The last visit, however, resulted in a near disaster when, after work, Mark decided to try to swim across the lake in front of their home. Ken's wife, Ramona, was frantic because Mark ignored her pleas to get out of the water. Ken had to go out and bring him back to shore. That was the final straw. Mark rarely returned to Smith Mountain.

Even Chris (who has six children) with his wife Suellen took Mark for several weeks. Mark seemed to fit in with the clan until he decided to help discipline the children. This did not fare well with Chris's children. The few weeks had gone well, but it was enough for Chris and his family; Mark was brought home.

All of the brothers even took Mark on a weekend bass fishing trip in 1994. The "boys" came back with stories that had us laughing for days. My brothers' antics made for salacious yarns as each sibling embellished his own slant into fish tale proportions! Between their accounts of being caught in a horrendous thunderstorm and luring Mark out of the boat, the whole family wondered how they arrived home in one piece.

Mark seemed to enjoy the unique variety of adventures with each of his siblings. Every time a brother or sister came home for a visit Mark would pack his bags and say, "I go with you," It didn't matter where he went, he loved each and every adventure that took him away from the daily chores of the farm.

For several weeks during the summers beginning in 1997, I shouldered responsibility for my brother. The timing was prefect since I was a teacher and had more flexibility during the summer. I actually looked forward to being with Mark during my vacation. I worked hard planning activities and places to go. One year we took him with us to the beach, which he loved. Mark was proud each year to bring home an album full of photos taken during his vacation in Nashville. He entertained visitors to the Simpson home with his photo albums.

During these two- or three-week periods, Mark was a full-time job which was about all my marriage or I could endure. My husband Clark had a stressful job and needed to be totally relaxed at home. With Mark around, Clark was always worried: where was he, what did he need, and what was he up to. Being with Mark required great patience. We tended to treat him as a baby brother, a five-year-old. To think of him as an adult with rights and the right to make choices was a challenge. We attempted to give him a margin of freedom, but invariably an incident would occur and we reverted to parental approaches, administering discipline instead of treating him more as a peer. We were too emotionally involved.

My sister, Dianna, had the best coping skills to deal with Mark. At times he listened to and obeyed her better than he did my parents. So it was a relief for me when for several years Dianna and her husband Allan offered to drive Mark the nine-hour trip to Nashville. Dianna and I are not only sisters, we're best friends. Her visits allowed us time together as well helping to care for our brother. Wanting to find fun activities for Mark, my husband suggested we try to enroll him in a camp. A new camp had opened and even provided transportation from the nearby YMCA. This would give Mark a fun-packed day in an outdoor center that provided a wide variety of activities. We spoke with the director who decided that as long as Mark did not have a behavior problem, he would be welcome. The director was open to inclusion, and could not have been kinder in welcoming my brother for a few weeks at camp.

Camp was an immediate hit with Mark. He loved the activities; he loved being a camper! Whenever we came to Virginia, Mark would immediately greet us, point his finger at me and say, "I go with you." Although we were not always able to grant his wish, the times he went home with us are ones I now treasure, forever pressed in my memory as the happiest of times.

Research on siblings indicates that there are positive aspects in being the sibling of a brother or sister with a disability. Researchers have found that children in families where a sibling has a disability can become more mature, responsible, self-confident, independent and patient. These siblings can also become more altruistic (charitable), more sensitive to humanitarian efforts and have a greater sense of closeness to family (Lobato, 1990; Powell, 1993)

Rick Berkobien, "Siblings: Brothers and Sisters of People Who Have Mental Retardation," copyright 1995-2003, accessed online at The Arc, http://www.nas.com/downsyn/siblings.html on July 12, 2004.
Reprinted with permission

Mark with his brothers after their fishing trip.

Mark was quite proud of his YMCA name tag.

All adults make choices on a daily basis, from what to wear to work to where to spend the weekend. Adults with Down syndrome must be supported in their desire to make their own choices.

Dorothy Robison, Marty Wyngaarden Krauss, Marsha Mailick Seltzer, "Does Parenting Ever End?" Accessed at the National Down Syndrome Society (NDSS) website: www.ndss.org on January 15, 2004
Reprinted with permission

I Love Camp

No one knew. No one at the day camp knew how old Mark was when we asked that he be allowed to attend. Oh, they knew he wasn't six, twelve, or even fifteen. They didn't ask, so I didn't have to tell them that we were sending a camper who was forty-eight years old! No one ever asks for a mental age and Mark certainly fit in the five through eight year old age group, MENTALLY.

Camp was a Godsend for both Mark and me. Although I loved having my brother visit in the summer, it was exhausting. Unless he was within my peripheral vision, I was always worried about him. I didn't have to be concerned about five-year-olds anymore; my girls were grown and basically on their own. Mark's mental age of five somehow kept his forty-eight-year-old body young and just like a 5 year old, he could be mischievous. Keeping him busy and active was critical and camp was the answer.

Going to camp became my brother's idea of heaven. He simply could not wait to enjoy each day, whatever it brought. Camp was different than his normal routine and included swimming, one of his true loves. He could literally swim for hours. I cannot fathom how his aging body never seemed to tire in the water, and I was envious of his stamina. One of his favorite spots was the camp's spanking new water park. This portion of the recreation area was a wonderland of waterworks. Mark's favorite seemed to be the giant tubes that had masses of water pouring out like a pipe that had just burst. He loved to stand under the cylinder and let water smash down on his head. I kept wondering why the force of the water didn't knock him flat to the bottom of the pool.

I remember the first time Mark had to sign up for the various activities offered at camp. Our friend, Dan Schlacter, happened to be a counselor and to our pleasant surprise, Mark was assigned to his group. I felt all would be well with Dan watching over him and I was right except when it came to activity sign-ups. When Mark handed his sign-up list to me, I gasped!

"Dan, how did you let Mark sign up for THESE activities?" I asked.

"Well, it was his choice," he nonchalantly stated. "I think I remember him saying 'Hey, I wanna do that'."

"You know Mark cannot read, Dan. I'm sure he didn't mean to take Sign Language," I said. At the time I was not aware that some parents were teaching their young children with Down syndrome sign language to transition to speaking skills. I think Mark might have been too old for a camp sign language class.

"Oops, well that can be changed," he laughed.

Dianna (who had driven Mark to Nashville) and I were skeptical of archery to say the least. We both had visions of him directing his "Marks"manship toward an unsuspecting camper. Dan thought Mark would be just fine.

We knew fishing and swimming would be his favorites. Add to that basketball and Mark would have everything needed for a successful camping experience.

The last item on his list was the alpine tower, a ninety-foot climbing apparatus. Kids and adults alike love the tower, but we knew Mark was afraid of heights!

Later, we found that Mark was taken out of sign language and instead went to an extra basketball session. This was one of his favorite sports, and he could score more baskets than most campers. When he went to the alpine tower, he rested on the picnic table and watched the other climbers, never once showing any desire to conquer his fear of heights. Archery was our biggest surprise. We were told that Mark took the class, loved it, and became a decent archer.

We felt positive about that first day, and Mark was positive that he wanted to return. He was not only the oldest camper, he was the happiest.

Although my brother had a passion for the water and camp, getting him organized each day just to attend was an ordeal. The challenge was to get him ready and drive each morning to a central pick-up point at the local YMCA where other eager campers would join him to be transported to the day camp site thirty minutes away.

The test was to encourage my brother to hustle, as he was slow-paced. Getting him up and out of the bed in the morning took a good hour. If left alone, you would expect that within an hour he would have his clothes on, teeth brushed, and so on. Not so! You could never depend on him to be punctual. After spending any time at all with Mark, you realized there were only two options:

1. Just presume that time will not be an issue.

2. Stay with him and dress him.

Obviously, the latter proved to be a necessity if we were to get to the bus on time. To hasten the process, I began to prepare the night before. I had to allow at least thirty minutes for a shower as he was exhilarated by the feeling of water splashing onto his skin. Mark took so much time bathing that I learned quickly showers must become a nightly versus a morning event. He sometimes got out of the shower, dressed, and then returned to the shower for a second time! I knew he would never tire of being in water.

Shaving was another matter of concern. Mark loved to shave, so much so that he would actually get red razor burns on his face from overuse. After his night shave I had to hide the razor. If it wasn't concealed Mark would be shaving on the way to catch the bus.

That done, I made sure shorts, underwear, T-shirts, were beside the bed. Laying his clothes out the night before avoided the problem of repeated wearings. My brother became fanatical about items he liked, wearing them every day. It didn't matter if they had odors or muddy spots, he never seemed to tire of them.

To hasten the dressing process in the morning, I literally helped Mark put on each piece of clothing. On his own he would s-l-o-w-l-y put on one sock, then something would distract him. It could be a fly in the room, but the diversion consumed valuable time.

The morning schedule had to include a litany of procedures, carefully timed:

—get Mark up (he had been known to stay in bed all day with a cover over his head)

— make sure necessities were taken care of (face washed, teeth brushed)

—run downstairs and dress myself

—run back up and help Mark dress

—run down again to get lunch ready

—back up to get Mark and his backpack

—rush back down the stairs and out the door

Finally with the checklist complete, I grabbed his lunch and out the door we went.

If I promised coffee, Mark seemed to pick up the pace a bit. Finally making it to the car, we zoomed away.

One morning I was left with my husband's Miata convertible. As cute as that car was, I hated it. I had only slightly mastered the stick shift in driver's education years ago. The car's clutch was an antiquated apparatus to me and my driving showed it.

Mark is quite fond of coffee so we stopped for his morning treat. My brother thought he was "hot stuff" in the convertible. Wildly waving at every car and passer by, he pointed to the sports car and said, "Hey, I want one of these." As we drove on, I glanced at Mark who by now was sitting proudly with his coffee, as though he owned the car and I was his chauffeur.

Changing gears has always been my biggest challenge with stick shifts. This morning I had a particularly difficult time. As I switched gears, I went directly from first to third: jump, sputter, jump, lurch, jump, sputter, lurch.

"Damn," I said, trying to find first gear again. Of course, I am doing this with my own coffee in one hand! Why didn't this sports car have cup holders? As I tried to control the lurching car, I looked at Mark, who had his cup three feet above the car with his arm as far out of the auto as possible.

"Hey," he said, pointing to his T-shirt. My gear shift had caused Mark's coffee to splash out, creating un-sightly brown splotches. His face revealed disgust, and then he uttered one huge sigh.

I laughed, "What a way to start a morning, uh, Mark? You're ok, the camp bus is waiting and maybe YOU should drive next time!"

My brother obviously stood out at camp, yet he was treated as "one of the guys." The counselors were easygoing and relaxed with Mark. Perhaps their example allowed my brother to be so readily accepted by the campers. Everyone was very friendly and made Mark feel at home. He went from one activity to another with his group, enjoying his chosen activities as well as extra pastimes which included everything from horseback riding to kayaking, to swimming.

Less than a week after camp began, whenever we entered the parking lot, it was clear everyone knew this guy.

"Hi, Mark!"

"Hey ya, Mark!"

"Mark, how's it goin?"

One mom tenderly stopped me and told me that her little boy had said, "Oh, Mom, there's the old man that still likes to play."

The concept of inclusion may be viewed as a progression or continuum with varying levels of acceptance... The highest level, social inclusion, refers to individuals' abilities to gain acceptance and have positive interactions with peers. Full inclusion in recreation results when programs are welcoming, accommodating, and conducive to sharing experiences.

Marcia J. Carter, Katy M. McCown, S. Forest, J. Martin, et al. "Exercise and Fitness for Adults with Developmental Disabilities: Case Report of a Group Intervention," *Therapeutic Recreation Journal*, Vol. XXXVIII, No. 1, pp. 72-84, June 2, 2004. Reprinted with permission

...we found that many adults with Down syndrome rely on self-talk to vent feelings such as sadness or frustration. They think out loud in order to process daily life events. This is because their speech or cognitive impairments inhibit communication.

Dennis McGuire, PhD, Brian A. Chicoine, MD, and Elaine Greenbaum, PhD, "Self-Talk" in Adults with Down Syndrome, Disability Solutions, Vol. 2, Issue 2, pp. 1-5, July/August, 1997. Reprinted with permission

Goin' to Nashville

We were not sure when Mark began talking to himself. We were not sure if he could control this self-talk. We WERE sure that it drove everyone nuts!

When my brother thought he was alone he would begin talking to himself. Only occasionally could we decipher what he was saying. Sometimes it sounded like unintelligible garble, other times his emotions ran high as he loudly mumbled his discontent with someone or some incident.

Mixed in with his mumbling, sometimes Mark would find a catch phrase and we would hear continuous repetitions of that phrase for days, weeks, and sometimes months. Just like the "call the sheriff" mantra, the phrase usually related to someone or something he had heard. For example, when he was going to visit us, he repeated "goin' to Nashville, goin' to Nashville, goin' to Nashville, GOIN' TO NASHVILLE" getting louder with each repetition, sounding like an incoherent raging preacher! Even when he arrived in Nashville, he still repeated "goin' to Nashville." When we asked him to stop, he put his finger to his mouth signaling that he would not mumble, but it usually did not last.

When Mark was outside at the farm, he let it all out and pontificated to the whole world. Only the cows occasionally looked up as they chewed their cud. I could imagine them saying, "Hey, Martha, look, the guy who talks to himself is back outside. Love to know who he's mad at."

Mark also loved to use the bathroom as a refuge or pulpit. He locked the door and ranted with few interruptions. When he visited one summer, a distant uncle of my husband's passed away. Because we knew no one who would feel comfortable "babysitting" Mark, he had to travel with us to the wake. The three-hour drive was uneventful except for the stop at a Cracker Barrel™ restaurant, one of his favorites.

"Hey," he poked me from the back seat when he spotted the Cracker Barrel logo. After several such nudges, we conceded and stopped to eat. He loved their home cooked food and especially savored the taste of their coffee.

When we arrived at the wake in Washington, Indiana, he was happy, content, and full, but he knew no one in the small, aged funeral home. There was no television, no basketball, nothing in the place to interest him. He didn't want to be there. He was bored.

Mark discovered the bathroom (the only one in the funeral parlor) and headed in that direction as the evening prayer service commenced.

Softly the priest began to lead us in prayer. "Let us bow our heads. Lord, we pray for your faithful servant."

"All this crap, all this crap, all this traffic, I want sunshine, I go home, goin to Nashville, goin to Nashville," came the loud mumbling from the bathroom! The interruption was creating quite a commotion. Mark had started his self-talk, saying he wanted out of this place and God only knows what else. The good news was that little of what Mark yelled out was understood, but the guests were aghast.

"Who in the heck was disturbing the service?" they obviously wondered.

My husband knew and rushed to the bathroom door. "Mark, open this door!" he said in the loudest whisper he could muster.

No response.

"Mark, I've got you a cup of coffee."

Coffee. That word alone could get us out of tight situations. Mark found coffee irresistible and the utterance alone stopped his bathroom bedlam.

Slowly the door creaked open. Clark stood there with a cup of java in his hand.

"Yeah coffee," Mark smiled.

Clark put a finger up to his mouth so that Mark understood that he needed to be quiet. Giving him the coffee had a calming effect, allowing the ceremony to continue without further interruption.

We smiled to ourselves that Mark had been loud enough to rattle a number of older guests and to almost wake the dead!

I think all of this was simply his way of venting frustrations. Many of us can vent aggravations and concerns to friends or family, but because of Mark's inability to speak clearly, his self-talk became his way of venting. I had noticed, however, that even when he was happy, he mumbled. When he would go to the bath house at camp, thinking he was alone, he often began loud incessant mumbling sessions. The bath house had open air vents high above the doors, magnifying and broadcasting the noise. The entire camp heard him.

There seemed to be one place where Mark never mumbled. My parents knew they could have a silent moment from Mark every Sunday for one hour at their little Catholic church on a hill in Virginia, St. Victoria's. I guess Mark knew that he did not have to speak in church because God heard him and was taking care of him. In this holy place, Mark somehow knew he was safe. He was at peace.

That adults with Down syndrome use self-talk to cope, to vent, and to entertain themselves should not be viewed as mental illness. Self-talk may be one of the few tools available to adults with Down syndrome for asserting control over their lives and improving their sense of well-being.

Dennis McGuire, PhD, Brian A. Chicoine, MD, and Elaine Greenbaum, PhD, "Self-Talk" in Adults with Down Syndrome, Disability Solutions, Vol. 2, Issue 2, pp. 1-5, July/August, 1997. Reprinted with permission

The concrete nature of the thought processes of most people with Down syndrome is very functional and can be very precise if allowed to flourish in an appropriate setting. Often people with Down syndrome do wonderfully in jobs that have concrete tasks. The challenge for many people with Down syndrome comes when a task changes and they must take what they learned and apply it to a new situation.

Dennis McGuire, Ph.D. & Brian Chicoine, M.D., *Mental Wellness in Adults With Down Syndrome*, (Bethesda, MD: Woodbine House, 2006). Reprinted with permission

Now You Tell Me!

Mark could never speak clearly. When all of us were home, we adjusted to his language patterns and could understand a good deal of what he spoke. After I left home, it was apparent to me that either Mark's speech had worsened or I simply had lost touch with his speech habits. Many times I could only decipher a few words. My parents could understand him to a point, but even they occasionally misunderstood. If Mark could get away with it, he just pointed to what he wanted.

My theory was that after all these years, he had tired of trying to be understood. I compare his situation to that of a stroke victim who cannot articulate words, even though thoughts are in the brain, struggling to get out. I remember that total frustration myself when I had encephalitis and was having a seizure. An intuitive nurse said, "You're trying to speak but it won't come out will it, Honey?" Her empathy and recognition were comforting.

It would be fascinating to look at life through Mark's eyes. He had a world in his brain that I can only imagine.

When he did "crazy" things, it all seemed quite logical in his eyes.

Mark reasoned, perceived, and expressed himself at a different level. The onus was on US to accept and try to understand.

Mark was very clever, however, and could make the best of miscommunication. His inability to articulate clearly what he wanted or what he understood opened up the opportunity to interpret communication anyway HE wanted it.

One such misunderstanding created problems for Mark at camp on "share your lunch" day. He presented me with a note explaining that each camper was assigned a food item to share with his group. Pleased that my brother remembered to give me the paper, I read that we were to donate brownies, an easy treat to prepare. Happy to contribute, I baked the night before the sharing event, even garnishing the goodies with chocolate frosting. Mark was passionate about food and especially sweets. He watched me place the brownies in a portable carrier like Sylvester the Cat, licking his chops in anticipation of a fine dinner of Tweety Bird!

"Mark, you cannot eat these brownies, understand? You can have one at lunch, but first give them to your counselor," I reminded him.

He nodded his head.

I could tell he wasn't "tuned in." The smell of freshly baked brownies was distracting. He knew about noontime and how the system worked. Campers brought their own lunch with each group eating to-gether in their own little wooded space. Sharing had not been part of the routine.

The next morning I helped Mark out the door, re-peating the instructions: "Give the brownies to your counselor. Give the brownies to your counselor."

That afternoon when Mark stepped off the bus, I was slightly disappointed to see about half the dessert still in the pan. I couldn't understand as active boys would normally devour anything sweet.

"Mark, did everyone like the brownies?" I asked.

"Yep."

I spoke with his counselor, John, the next day only to find out that Mark WOULD NOT SHARE HIS brownies. He had enjoyed what the other boys had brought, but decided that the delectable treat he brought was his alone. When I discovered this, I made a new batch of brownies and brought them to the counselor's meeting the next day. Mark handed the brownies to the counselor himself and apologized.

"You were supposed to give these brownies to the counselor to share with all of your new friends," I pointed out.

Mark grins at me as though as he finally understood the directive I had repeatedly given the day before and said, "Now you tell me!"

Research tells us that people with Down syndrome experience a significant difference between what they *understand,* and what they are able to *communicate.*

Joan E. Medlen, R.D. "Did You say Something...or Were You Just Talking to Yourself?" *Disability Solutions,* July/August, 1997, Volume 2, Issue 2, pg. 2.
Reprinted with permission

New Year's Eve 2004 - Mark with his sisters and father.

Down syndrome is not related to race, nationality, religion or socioeconomic status. The most important fact to know about individuals with Down syndrome is that they are more like others than they are different.

"Facts about Down Syndrome," accessed online at www.nads.org on April 23, 2005.
Reprinted with permission

I'm So Upset

Mark's usual joviality and upbeat attitude could be drastically altered if his environment was in turmoil. One summer while Mark was visiting, my teenage daughter and I had occasional altercations. They were typical adolescent situations, but I sometimes came to Caroline's juvenile level rather than react as an adult with good sense. During one squabble, we were practically screaming at each other with biting words and rude expressions. Both of us were fuming when things subsided and we went about other household tasks. As I climbed the steps to collect dirty clothes, I was shocked to find Mark with his suitcase ready to head down the stairs to the front door.

"What are you doing with that suitcase? Where are you going?"

"I'm so upset!"

"Whatever for?" (Mark was always happy to visit. He never wanted to leave.)

"All that noise, I'm, I'm so upset, upset, upset!"

Then the reality of the last encounter with Caroline hit me. Mark had heard us yelling, and was so disturbed that he was just going to leave.

"Oh, my gosh, Mark, I'm so sorry. Caroline, come here and look at this," I called to my daughter.

When Caroline arrived, she saw her uncle with his luggage.

"Because of our yelling, Mark wants to leave," I said. "Mark, we are not mad at each other. We were just having a little spat. See?" I showed him that we were fine as Caroline and I gave each other a hug.

"Mark, here, let's take that suitcase back," Caroline gently spoke. "We don't want you to leave. We love you. We're so sorry we upset you." We each gave him a hug.

With tears in our eyes, we stood there realizing that Mark had just taught US a lesson. I do not recall why we were fighting, but I do remember how our actions and words affected a gentle spirit that day. It made us see the absurdity of our squabble. If our unkind utterances had hurt Mark, they had to be damaging to each of us. It brought us back to the reality that we truly loved each other and needed to treat each other with respect. Mark was OUR teacher that day.

Some of our patients seem to be sensitive to activity going on around them that others might just "tune out." This can lead to sensory overload. ...many of our patients seem to be sensitive to activities that are going on a distance from them that do not involve them. This awareness of activity is present even when the person doesn't appear to be paying attention. ...Loud noises, overly stimulating environments, and other "sensory overload" can cause the person to become upset, agitated, anxious, or depressed.

Dennis McGuire, Ph.D. and Brian Chicoine, M.D., Mental Wellness in Adults with Down Syndrome, A Guide to Emotional and Behavioral Strengths and Challenges, (Bethesda, MD: Woodbine House, 2006)
Reprinted with permission

> Enhancing the adulthood status of the individual requires decreasing family influence as the skills of the individual increase. Families are more reluctant to release their influence.

Cheryl Hanley-Maxwell, "Families: The Heart of Transition." Accessed at the National Down Syndrome Society (NDSS) website: www.ndss.org on July 12, 2004. Reprinted with permission

I Need a Haircut!

Mark has always had a fetish about cutting his hair. Sometimes when we visited Virginia, his hair line was very uneven.

"Mark, what happened to your hair?" we asked, but he shook his head and looked at us as if he was sorry we had brought the matter up.

"Oh, he got a hold of the scissors, again!" Mom would inform us unhappily.

My parents were careful to hide the scissors, but once in awhile, he found them.

I had forgotten this idiosyncrasy when he visited one summer. In an effort to keep Mark busy, I had bought him a scrapbook where he could place pictures of his vacation in Nashville. Sensing that he was bored I grabbed the scrapbook, a few magazines, and the scissors.

"Here, Mark, look what you can do. Cut pictures out of the magazines that you like and put them in your scrapbook," I told him.

He looked at me and smiled. He must have thought: " *Are you kidding, you're giving ME scissors?* "

I left him, smugly thinking that I had discovered a new fun and educational activity. I would share the idea with Mom and Dad to use when Mark was bored. When I came back to check on his progress, he had cut out a picture of the sun. He particularly liked the MasterCards™ as, to him, it looked like the sun on the front. He also cut out a jet skier.

"All right, Mark, great job! Now we'll just put these in your scrapbook. Keep going!" I said with enthusiasm.

I resumed my chores and was pleased that I did not have to constantly be by his side. This new activity would allow me more time to get my work done.

When I went back to check on my ward, I noticed little hairs strewn around the couch where he was "scrapbooking." I looked at his face, and there was a huge chunk of hair gone from his head!

The project abruptly ended.

I shrieked, "Mark, darn it, look at this mess, look at your hair!"

"W-w-e-ll, I need a haircut!"

I realized too late that if Mark had access to scissors, he would use them and become his own self-proclaimed barber.

My smug self-satisfaction of allowing my brother to be alone with scissors had backfired. I pulled from my educational background tools that I felt would give Mark an activity that would keep him busy as well as provide practice working with manipulatives. I thought working with the scissors would also help improve his fine motor skills and he would be so engrossed with this pastime that I could trust him as I carried out other chores around the house. I had good intentions, but Mark's rare moment alone with a pair of scissors was too tempting. He "needed" a haircut and that superceded cutting pictures from a magazine!

My parents had wisdom beyond my educational expertise. They would have said, "I told you so."

I don't even think I told them about the lesson I learned about leaving Mark alone with scissors.

Individuals with Down syndrome may have difficulty freeing themselves from the role of a child, but not yet be fully equipped to assume the responsibilities of a mature adult. Hence, this can be a troublesome transition for those having normal intellectual abilities.….Many young people with Down syndrome have most of the physical attributes of normal youngsters, but they often lack the cognitive and behavioral capabilities to cope with either the demands of the environment or their own desire for independence. Leisure activities are a vital aspect in the fulfillment of life for people with Down syndrome.

Siegfried M. Pueschel, "Young People with Down Syndrome: Transition from Childhood to Adulthood." Accessed at the National Down Syndrome Society (NDSS) website: www.ndss.org on July 12, 2004. Reprinted with permission

Mark enjoys a moment with his niece. Jacqueline lived close by and probably spent more time with Mark than any of our parent's grandchildren.

Down syndrome occurs in one out of every 733 live births, and more than 350,000 people in the U.S. have this genetic condition. One of the most frequently occurring chromosomal abnormalities, Down syndrome affects people of all ages, races and economic levels.

National Down Syndrome Society (NDSS), "General Information." Accessed online at www.ndss.org on October 28, 2006.

McDonalds™

It was going to be a unique evening for my mother's seventieth birthday. My sister and five brothers all had secretly arrived in Nashville from out of state to participate in the celebration. The plan was to have a white stretch limousine whisk my parents and three of her sisters (who also had come for the surprise) from their hotel to various Nashville popular downtown sites, where her seven children had each been strategically placed. At every stop one by one we would join my surprised mother, presenting her with a rose. Mom, who had not ridden in a limo since her wedding more than fifty years ago, was already aglow with excitement!

Waiting for mother's arrival with Mark would be my seventeen-year-old daughter, Caroline. The downtown site we selected for Mark would be McDonalds, his favorite eatery. When he spied the golden arches, it was all over, he had to go to "McDonalds, McDonalds, McDonalds"! Mark was obsessed with this fast food eatery and particular about his visits. Drive-thru's were unacceptable; he truly loved to take his time and dine inside!

Mark was all smiles as he and Caroline walked into McDonald's®, looking like a homeless couple. Caroline was wearing faded tattered jeans and an over-sized sloppy vintage top purchased from Goodwill. Mark too was dressed casually in a favorite t-shirt. After traveling eight hours from Virginia for this shindig, he saw no reason to change. In his hand, which was bandaged from an injury on the farm, he clutched a rose I had given him to present to mom. It was becoming a bent-over, gasping-for-breath rose, due to my brother's firm grip.

"Mark, would you like something to eat? Caroline asked, knowing his response would be positive. Immediately her uncle pointed to a Big Mac. My daughter rummaged through her pockets but found little money.

"Can I help you, ma'am?" asked the girl behind the counter, looking at the misfits with disdain. In this area of the city one could find an array of strange, unorthodox people including aspiring songwriters, down and out, waiting to be "found." The homeless of the city also walked around, sometimes sleeping on the sidewalks near fast food restaurants. I'm sure this McDonald's® employee was no stranger to disadvantaged folks coming in and asking for food. When Caroline and Mark walked in, it appeared that they were having tough times.

"I want hamburger and those," said Mark, pointing to a picture of crispy French fries and a frosty coke.

Caroline double-checked her pockets. In her rush to drive to McDonalds she had forgotten to bring her purse. She gathered whatever she could find in her holey jeans.

The clerk stood impatiently waiting, "Can I help you?" she repeated loudly in a disgusted tone.

"Ummm, look, what can I buy for $2.45? It's all I have," Caroline whispered in embarrassment.

A paradigm shift resulted in a changed expression that came over the woman's face. She looked at Caroline with her frayed clothes and then she glanced at

Mark. It was obvious these two were in worse shape than she thought.

Her voice softened, "Don't you worry about a thing, Honey. What would you like?"

"I'm fine, but my uncle would love a Big Mac, fries, and a Coke," Caroline said in her sweetest voice.

"Coming up," she smiled. Even the tone in her voice changed.

In a few moments the clerk returned with a Big Mac combo for Mark, adding fries and a drink for Caroline.

"No charge," she said sympathetically. She had done her good deed for the day.

Caroline, pleasantly surprised, thanked the clerk and led her uncle to a booth. Mark was hungry and happily began to consume his supersized hamburger. Being a man who takes his time, Caroline had to hasten his dining experience as she knew Mom and the birthday clan would soon arrive.

One can only imagine the look on the employee's face when a stretch white limousine pulled into the fast food parking lot. WHO in this restaurant would be riding in such class?

"Mark, let's go, here's our ride!" Caroline exclaimed as she rushed to collect what was left of his mini-feast and deposit it in the trash.

The clerk who had befriended the "homeless" couple was flabbergasted as she watched them walk out and head for the limousine.

Mark stepped into the limo and greeted Mom with his rose. He surveyed the elaborate interior of this swanky car, something he had never seen before. It was huge and included snacks, pretty lights, and soft drinks!

"Hey, I want one of these," he remarked, immediately gliding into one of the seats.

Staring out of the McDonald's® window was one shocked employee. To see a "homeless" guy to whom she had just given a free meal get into a limousine must

This photograph was taken at the McDonald's near the group
home in Virginia where Mark was a regular customer.

have exceeded her wildest imaginations. I wonder if
she will ever feel compassion for anyone helpless again.

The joy that day brought to my mother was unforgettable. She had the best gift, her family was together
sharing a milestone in her life. Having Mark with us
was critical. He has always been an integral part of our
lives in all the celebrations and significant shared
events. He was indispensable.

Mark, oblivious to what had just occurred, simply
enjoyed his best trip ever——leaving McDonalds in style!

It's time now to see that people with disabilities enjoy full participation
in our communities. Parents have to help others abandon their odd
notions about people with disabilities and begin to see them the way
we do: as warm, giving individuals. The only way that will happen is if
people come together, one-by-one, face-to-face.

Linda Stengle, M.H.S., "Why Bother? Networking An Adult
Child with Disabilities," Disability Solutions, Vol. 2, Issue 2, pg. 14,
July/August, 1997. Reprinted with permission

In the continuing role of extended family members in the quality of life of individuals with Down syndrome, family bonds bend to the changing life circumstances and opportunities of individuals with Down syndrome.

Dorothy Robison, Marty Wyngaarden Krauss, Marsha Mailick Seltzer, "Does Parenting Ever End?," National Down Syndrome Society (NDSS). Accessed online at www.ndss.org, May 19, 2003.
Reprinted with permission

Steve and Nancy

In the 1990s, it was more and more apparent that Mark no longer wanted to live on the farm. He loved activity and going places. Our parents, by then in their seventies, were very content to enjoy their home. None of the activities there interested my brother. He would carry out household chores, but he had loved getting up and going to work in town at a "real" job. No longer allowed at the local sheltered workshop, Mark had no where else to go but home.

Mark also chafed more under Dad's strict discipline for misbehavior. He wanted more freedom, not atypical of any maturing human being seeking some sort of independence. In this light, Mark was becoming more difficult to manage. He continued his minor antics such as sneaking Cokes, eating too much, staying up late, as well as outright disobedience such as locking himself in his room. Then he began walking, just meandering down the country roads. This added worry and stress to my parents. They had to search for him, never knowing where they might find their wayward son. Once they found him a mile away on his bike with a suitcase on the front handlebars, trying to manage (with difficulty) this cumbersome baggage while attempting to steer.

"Goin' to Nashville," he stated as the truck pulled up. Plunking the bicycle into the back of the truck, Mark was carted back home. This was his way of crying out; he wanted out of the situation. When siblings offered to care for him, it was a relief to both Mark and his parents.

Going to my brother Steve and his wife Nancy's was one of his favorite retreats. They drove three hours from their home in North Carolina to retrieve Mark. While they visited with my parents, Mark sat in the car for hours just to make sure he didn't miss his ride with "Steve and Nancy." Overall he was a great traveler, content if you fed him, occasionally rewarding him with a diet coke or decaf coffee.

Nancy is a nurse anesthetist with a heart of gold. She was exceptionally patient and understanding with Mark. Perhaps her nursing background was partly responsible for her nurturing and caring nature, yet, she was no pushover and would not put up with any non-sense. Mark knew she genuinely loved him. He really enjoyed being with Nancy and had an open invitation to walk with her each morning. Being fond of outdoor exercise, he was happy to tag along.

One noteworthy morning Nancy decided to jog alone, letting Mark sleep in. She did not realize that her brother-in-law had decided to follow her, although he was walking in the wrong direction. She returned just in time to dress for work. Before heading out the door she checked to see if Mark was still sleeping, but the bed was empty! After scouring the house, Steve and Nancy decided to drive around the area to find him. It wasn't long before they spied him, walking aimlessly along the lake looking for Nancy. They were relieved and upset all at the same time. Nancy never jogged again before first checking on Mark's whereabouts.

Sometimes Steve took Mark to the beach and let him fish or swim. On one such excursion Steve told Mark he could go out and swim in the ocean, but Mark shook

Mark and his niece, Caroline, enjoying a day at the lake. He loved his vacations with us in Nashville

As a groomsman (far left in photo) in his brother Ken's wedding. Mark has fun teasing before the ceremony.

Mark and I loved to dance.

Mark photographed with his niece, Megan, who works with autistic children.

My daughters, Christin and Caroline, are shown here with Mark at my father's 80th birthday party. It was to be the last family party that my brother would attend.

Mark and I both enjoyed lounging by the pool enjoying the Florida sun.

Caroline, who now teaches special education, with Mark in Florida.

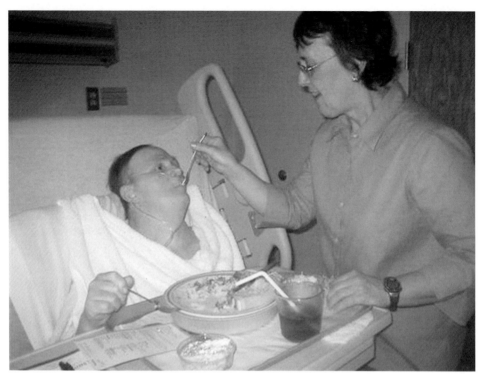

Mark's sister-in-law, Nancy, helps out in the hospital.

Nephew's Jean Paul and Daniel Lavoie, who attended high school at Hargrave Military Academy, are standing at attention with Mark.

This is a collage of pictures I made for Mark after his three week vacation in the summer of 1998. The photos reveal some of my brother's favorite activities.

I spoiled my brother with a bubble bath. He thought he was a king, even enjoying a cup of coffee among the suds!

My parents proudly stand next to Mark after his graduation from The Simpson Farm School.

A collage of photos showing a few of Mark's camping experiences in Nashville.

Mark loved sledding when
he lived on the farm.

Mom helps Mark as he plays Bingo.

his head. My brother couldn't believe the negative reaction; Mark loved to swim. He pointed to his wrist which was sporting a new birthday watch. Realizing he didn't want to get it wet, Steve offered to hold it while he swam. This would not suffice. Mark would not part with his timepiece. Even though he was unable to tell time, Mark believed he COULD. This watch also had a button, which illuminated the display. Mark loved that aspect, and his own face lit up each time he pressed that button. Somehow knowing water might ruin his "glowing watch," crossing the threshold into the ocean was not an option.

"Mark, get out there and swim, or I'll take you out myself," my impatient brother commanded. So, Mark hesitatingly walked out into the ocean. A few moments later, Steve looked up to check on Mark. Scanning the ocean, he could not see his brother. A shot of panic struck! Steve knew he had only taken a fleeting look away. It couldn't have been more than a few seconds. Anxiously, he searched once more, noticing something odd in the ocean-something poking out above the waves. It was an arm sticking straight out of the water, like a periscope from a submarine. But this periscope had a watch on it! Mark was swimming with one arm totally out of the ocean, the hand with his new watch. He did not want to get water on this prized possession.

Steve and Nancy helped with Mark on numerous occasions, caring for him for weeks at a time. Their daughters were older, which gave them more flexibility than other family members. The only major trouble came when they were getting ready to return Mark to the farm.

"I stay here," he would confidently state. Right around this time they noticed he became particularly helpful, sweeping and cleaning without being asked. He thought that being useful might allow the visit to be extended. In order to depart on time, eventually Steve and Nancy would have to fib and tell Mark they were going somewhere else. Upon arrival at the farm, he would sit in the car for hours, hoping to go back to North Carolina. He never unpacked his bags so that he'd always be ready in case there was an opportunity to go away with someone else.

Mark repeatedly would say, "Steve and Nancy" when he knew they were coming to visit and then for weeks after his unforgettable vacations to their cozy North Carolina home. We tired of hearing the repetitions, but he never tired of being with a brother and sister-in-law whom he dearly loved.

Persons with developmental disabilities non-service system supports are often siblings with whom they have maintained a life-long relationship.

Gary B. Seltzer, "Siblings: The Next Generation of Family Supports?", IMPACT (Institute on Community Integration College of Education, University of Minnesota) Vol. 6, no. 1, pg. 16, Spring 1993.
Reprinted with permission

Part III

I AM My Brother's Keeper!

Transition to a New Home

This was the last professional photograph taken of the family. The backdrop was an old barn that still stands and is situated near the farm house.

At the family farm, Mark's salute to the flag became a regular tradition.

For many adults with Down syndrome, having a home of their own is a lifelong dream. It is important to them to leave home and establish separate adult lives, just as their brothers and sisters do.

"Thank God, I'm a Country Boy"

It was a hit in 1975. John Denver's song, "Thank God, I'm a Country Boy," had everyone singing to the lyrics wherever they lived—city or country. It especially fit the little country farm of the Simpsons. Mark latched onto that song and it quickly became his theme. He loved saying, "Thank Go-d, I'm a Country Boy," drawing out the word "God." It became his motto as he loudly proclaimed many times a day that he was proud to be a country boy. And in those years (he was twenty-three when the song was released) Mark could not have been happier living on the farm. Just as the song's popularity diminished, Mark's desire to continue living on the farm slowly began to fade.

It had become readily apparent to us that Mark no longer wanted to live at home. Not long after my parents sold the recreation center, my brother Chris went away to college. Mark was now the only sibling left at home. Chris recounted that day:

I left in August of 1986, with my bike on the back of my car and mom in the driveway crying her eyes out. Mark stood next to her wondering why he couldn't go. It's interesting what you remember in your life and I vividly remember this scene. I also remember Mark seeing me pack my car and talking about how he was going to leave for college too. As I look back now, I can imagine being in Mark's shoes seeing the last child leave and wondering why he couldn't go too! He also saw his protector leaving. I stood up to Dad a couple of times when I thought he was being too strict with Mark and I know Mark remembers that. So not only was he being abandoned, but his advocate was leaving also, which I'm sure made it worse!

With Mark being the last sibling at home, he gradually became disgruntled and wanted to leave too. The frustration was exhibited through occasional outbursts of misbehavior.

My parents were grateful whenever we gave them a "break" from Mark whether for one day, a weekend, or two weeks. Respites were very acceptable, but, letting him leave forever was unthinkable.

It was an ongoing question, nagging in my subconscious—*who will become his care givers when my parents no longer are able?*

Since 1987, Mark had had a case worker from the state. This came about through the local Mental Retardation Services Office. This office is housed in the Community Services Board. Virginia Community Service Boards were organized in the late 1960s by geographical area and there are forty such boards in Virginia. According to the director of the local office, their mission is to be aware of those individuals with special needs and try to address their needs. These services are covered under Medicaid. Mom had called the community service office to inquire about the possibility of Mark working at the nearest workshop. She was referred to the mental retardation services division. The director told my mother there was a possibility of receiving case management services as well and she took the opportunity to have a case worker assigned to help with Mark's services.

Although state employees changed periodically, the various case workers for Mark visited frequently and I suppose they felt things were going well or simply accepted my parents' wish not to pursue other avenues of housing for Mark. My sister had investigated nearby group homes and was quite impressed with the activities and the care provided for those with special needs. Dianna suggested to Mom and Dad that they look at options for Mark. They went so far as to put him on a waiting list for the possibility of moving to a group home, a positive move for my reluctant parents. Yet we found it strange that Mark's name never made it to the top of the list.

"Mom, where is Mark on the list?" I would inquire. "Have you called and checked?"

"I don't know," she would mumble. "I guess they just put others ahead of him."

"You need to keep calling and checking, Mom, or you'll always be on the bottom of the list."

"I know, I'll do it next week."

I think in her heart she was not ready to let Mark go. This nurturing mother of seven was not ready for her last child to leave home, even if he was in his forties! Neither parent was trusting of any institution, feeling they were better caregivers. Dianna did finally get them to visit one group home. The group home housed a number of individuals with special needs. Each "consumer" had his or her own room. There was a full staff to help out twenty-four hours a day. Meals were prepared and activities planned. During the week residents were transported to a day support service where they could choose to color, work puzzles, exercise, or attend an array of goings-on in the local community. My parents and sister were very impressed with the staff, the cleanliness, and with activities available for the residents. Even after all of that, however, the time did not seem right.

"Mom, you are only 30 minutes away, you can visit him whenever you want," Dianna nudged her. The conversation stopped there. Mom had no interest in continuing...

We realized that patience would be the operative mode to deal with Mark's transition from home, but it was becoming more challenging because my brother was now physically stronger than my aging parents. If he didn't want to do something, it was pure hell to persuade Mark to obey. Occasional unpleasant altercations resulted between father and son. We knew the day would come in the non-so-distant future that, like a boiling tea kettle, the lid was bound to blow.

The evening the kettle blew, January 4, 2001, was frightening for my mother. It seems that Mark had sneaked a coke. Through trail and error, my parents had discovered that if Mark had caffeine or sugar, he tended to be more irritable; without consuming such goodies Mark was calmer and more affable. They began to limit such treats, especially at night as Mark would not sleep. Noticing my brother had taken a soft drink, Dad tried to grab it. Mark ran from him to the back of the house into the laundry room. Dad, in his stocking feet, bolted after him. While attempting to snatch the soft drink, his stocking feet slipped out from beneath him. He landed full body force on a step leading to the laundry area. Something cracked and Dad yelled out in pain, "Auugh, Ruth help!"

Mark, knowing he was in trouble, vaulted over Dad, flew past my mother up the stairs to his bedroom and promptly locked the door.

Mom was frantic. "Carroll, are you alright?" she screamed, her heart pounding.

"I can't move, I think I've broken something. Call the emergency squad!" My father continued moaning while lying there, his back throbbing in pain, as my mother called my sister, Dianna, and the ambulance.

Less than a quarter mile away, my sister rushed over

to help with the crisis. Knowing the rescue squad was on its way, Mom attended to her ailing husband and Dianna took charge of Mark. First she had to get him out of the bedroom.

The adrenalin was pumping as she demanded, "Mark, open this door!"

Gingerly, he turned the knob barely peeking through the crack. Shoving open the door, she took his hand firmly and led him downstairs.

My sister was visibly shaken and worried as they watched my father being prepped for transportation to the hospital. Dianna stood with Mark as their father was placed in the ambulance, red lights flashing. She hoped he understood that his father was seriously hurt. Mark then went with Dianna to the security of her home. This country boy who had always thanked God for his life on the farm, walked out that night never again to live with his mother and father.

The rescue squad immediately took my dad to a Lynchburg hospital where they diagnosed a badly broken hip. Immediate surgery was needed.

Although the operation went well, post-surgery was a disaster. Dad's catheter was incorrectly inserted, which caused an infection. He could have died the first night. We were grateful for our sister-in-law, Nancy, a nurse anesthetist, who had driven four hours when she heard of the accident. She took charge of the situation, staying with my mother and dad. After a few days, my father rapidly improved. The recuperation, however, would be lengthy. That is when my mother called me. She softly spoke into the phone, "Carolyn, I can't do this anymore."

"Eventually, all families, regardless of where the adult with Down Syndrome lives, must face the realization that they will not be available indefinitely to oversee the care and support of their adult child..."

Dorothy Robison, Marty Wyngaarden Krawss, Marsha Maitlick Seltzer, "Does Parenting Ever End?," Accessed online at the National Down Syndrome Society (NDSS) website: www.ndss.org on January 15, 2004. Reprinted with permission

Although the adult with Down syndrome and his parents may prefer that he live at home, the time will come when it is no longer possible for parents to be the primary caregivers.

Dorothy Robison, Marty Wyngaarden Krauss, Marsha Mailick Seltzer, "Does Parenting Ever End?." Accessed at the National Down Syndrome Society (NDSS) website: www.ndss.org on January 15, 2004. Reprinted with permission

I Stay Right Here

There are some phone calls one never forgets. That call from my mother told me she couldn't handle the stress of helping Dad recuperate and care for Mark at the same time. I could tell by the sound of her voice that my mother was ready to let Mark go. She had been so reluctant for all these years.

I'm sorry it took a crisis for her to realize that she couldn't take care of Mark any longer. She knew my father would need tremendous amounts of attention to recuperate and my mother would not leave his side. She did not need or want Mark to be a hindrance. I'm sure in her eyes, his behavior had started the entire situation. At this point Dianna told Mom, "Mark will never live with you and Dad again. Carolyn and I will handle it." Mom just hung her head and softly said, "Ok."

My father had always been the man in control. His military background taught him how to take command, and in his generation the man was always the authority in the family. Now this pillar of a man who was used to giving orders and making decisions was no longer in control. Because of his weak condition, my father was relieved to let his daughters take charge. When I arrived from Nashville Dianna and I told Dad that we were looking for a home for Mark. His humble and weak reply was, "I trust you girls."

Knowing that Dad had finally let go of Mark was of great comfort. A huge obstacle had been conquered. We began our search for Mark's new home, something he had been craving for years.

With my parents' blessing Dianna and I immediately took action. Steve and Dianna took turns letting Mark stay at their homes while we found a stable group residence. We knew this had to be temporary. No sibling was in a position to take Mark into his/her home permanently. Each had housed him for a few weeks at a time, but schedules and family dynamics made a permanent stay undesirable.

But where should Mark live? Who does one turn to at a time like this? We began with Mark's case worker. With her assistance, Dianna had done a lot of research before I arrived, getting places lined up to visit for possibilities for Mark's new home. His case worker had already moved Mark up to the top of the list for place-ment in a home. I took off work for a week and Dianna told me that she was so relieved to pick me up at the airport. She did not want to be left alone with major decisions, and my parents were in no condition mentally or physically to determine anything for Mark.

We thought the choice would be clear——a group home had been the number one possibility for several years. We were wrong. Now that a decision was imminent, we discovered other experts who believed that group homes were not as desirable as one or two people with special needs living in a small family setting; a house with one care giver. We had choices to make. We visited about three homes that were working that way, residential homes in a family setting. From the outside all looked to be viable options, and were within a thirty-minute drive of my parent's farm so they could visit Mark when they wanted. We were intrigued with one couple who lived in two different homes. The wife lived in a lovely home, caring for a woman with special needs. Not far away, her husband managed several young men with special needs in a home that had a farm setting. There were horses, chickens, fish, and an iquana! We immediately thought that this would be a perfect place for Mark. We liked the group home, but thought the atmosphere of the farm might be more conducive for our brother's new residence.

We returned home that day satisfied that the farm house was the place for Mark. Initially, he would probably have to stay at the wife's home until a space opened at the farm. The house had a swimming pool and a basket-ball stand in the back yard, so two of Mark's favorite pastimes would be readily available to him. The wife assured us that Mark living at the house would work because the two houses planned activities together. The list of activities looked like a wonderful climate in which to place my brother. We were anxious to get things moving.

That evening Dianna called the wife and left a message that we would like to place Mark in her family's residential setting. We thought within a week or two he could be happily adjusting to his new home. The message back was less enthusiastic. She would be gone to a conference for a week and then we could talk and see if Mark would work. There was an indefinite tone in her voice. We detected mixed signals. This delay was not good news. Mark was already working on two weeks at Dianna's and two weeks with Steve and Nancy. He needed roots and the family needed closure as to what was going to happen to our brother.

I began to sense that we were caught between philo-sophical views on caring for adults with special needs. Our case worker had to show us all options and allow US to make the decision. Group home advocates main-tained that when a crisis erupted in a small group setting there was no one to help out because there was usually only one caregiver in the home; also the caregiver in a single family home might leave and there would be total change requiring significant transition time. In a group home there were more caregivers, so that if anyone quit there were always numerous staff left, providing consistency for the adult with special needs. The smaller community supporters said the group homes were too institutional and many people with special needs liked the one-on-one care given in this family-type setting. Many people with special needs thrived well in this environment. Both of these possibilities were presented to us. It was important to have choices for Mark, but it certainly added another layer of complexity to our dilemma. All we wanted was what was best for our brother. We weren't emotionally prepared to deal with two philosophical points of view.

We both went back to meet with our state caseworker. That meeting was an eye opener for me. While she was complimentary about Mark's care, it was clear from our perspective that my parents had been avoiding making a decision about Mark. He could have gone to the group home years before. Dianna and I realized that Mark wanted to be treated more like an adult and my parents were treating him like a five-year-old child. The employees at the community service program gave choices and treated their "consumers" with the respect of an adult. Of course, Mark had to obey the rules, but they were far more flexible. If Mark wished to wear the same thing two or three times, he was allowed. If he wanted his hair cut, that would be his choice. If he didn't want to go somewhere, he could stay at the group home.

We were told Mark could not work at a workshop as he was labeled "high intensity" which meant he had to be supervised at all times. I think that was difficult for me to swallow as I always felt Mark could do some things independently; however, as I reflected on the times I watched Mark, he couldn't be trusted to stay in one place. He might walk away or get distracted and do something he shouldn't.

In her objective manner, the caseworker helped us to see clearly that Mark would be well cared for and that my parents and family could visit Mark anytime unannounced at the group home. There would be periodic conferences so that the family could give input. We began to realize that the truly best place for Mark would be the group home. None of us liked where it was located as part of the area looked rundown, but the home itself looked great. It was clean and well manicured. We were told there were good people living in the area. We also could get Mark into this home within two weeks.

My parents had left the decision entirely in our hands, and we prayed we would make the right choice. Resolution came when Dianna met the caseworker for a doctor's appointment with Mark. Dianna asked if she could take Mark to the group home after the appointment to see how he might react to living in this atmosphere. The caseworker felt this was a great idea. Upon arrival at the home, Mark immediately said, "I 'member this place." My sister discovered that three years earlier Mark had spent a day at the group home to see if this would be a future living possibility. He actually remembered the day clearly! As they entered the home Mark immediately took off his coat and said, "I stay right here."

"Thank you, Lord, for that sign," Dianna sighed looking upward toward heaven. That was it—the group home would be Mark's new residence.

We were warned that the transition would take a long time. Mark might not want to come home for awhile. We had lied so many times about taking him back to the farm that there was no trust. We would slowly have to rebuild this trust.

I had to return to work in Nashville, which left the moving day up to my sister. She went out and bought Mark new bedding and other necessities.

My sister tells me that the transition went remarkably well. Mark was so ready for this change! He loved his room. Dianna had found a comforter for his bed with basketballs on it and he settled into a routine enjoying the variety of activities and the attentive staff.

One of his favorite caregivers shared her first impressions of Mark.

> *I remember the first time I met Mark...He wanted a cup of coffee and the newspaper, and he walked the halls greeting everybody. At that moment I thought he was unique and funny. I told my co-workers, "I hope we get him in our group." I didn't have a clue that we would become best friends. I'm so grateful that you and Dianna chose our facility to place Mark, because if you hadn't, I would not have met him. He would not have been able to show me what real love is, unconditional love that doesn't cost anything, but time, and to be able to give love back. He was really a blessing to me.*

He spent the main part of his day at an adult day care center. He was happy there with numerous choices of leisure interests, and the van took the group to various places in the city—movies, concerts, malls, and so on. Mark had a schedule that would keep any of us on our toes!

One morning the van was ready to leave and because of his slow pace, he was not ready. He was told if he wasn't ready the van would have to leave. When Mark didn't come, that is precisely what happened!

"Hey, I want to go!" exclaimed Mark as he headed toward the door.

"Sorry, Mark, if you can't get ready in time, the van must leave. You'll have to stay here all day," remarked one of the staff members.

Mark looked at him but did not seem too concerned. He plopped himself down in front of the television and grabbed the remote control.

The staff member promptly turned off the TV.

"Mark, I'm sorry, but we don't watch television during the day. You'll have to do something else."

My stubborn brother sat there all day, all day, with the remote control in his hand! The staff allowed him, that was his choice. The next day Mark was ready to go in time for the van.

Mom and Dad visited each week and although he loved to see them, the first thing he said to them was "I love this place, I stay here." He wanted my parents to understand that he had no intention to return to the farm.

The first time that my parents came to the community service office for a conference with the caseworker and his new caregivers from the group home, the client (Mark) was to be included. The group home van arrived, Mark jumped out of the van and started running. He had to be chased. Mark had seen my parent's car and he was afraid that he was going to have to go back home. He was desperate to stay at the group home, so Mark returned to the van and was driven away. He would not be at the conference.

The good news was that Mark loved where he lived and he had no intention to return to the farm with my parents. My parents sat there so accepting. They had been through so much. They were getting so good at becoming detached from the situation. Seeing their special child thriving made them grateful; they loved Mark but were now keenly aware that he would never come back home. They realized this was good for them and for Mark.

Mark had to adjust to the other people with special needs in the group home. This gregarious guy would come up to the residents, put out his hand to shake it and say, "Hi, I'm Mark Simpson." Not everyone felt the same way about him. Many were not as agile as Mark. Some could barely walk. One African American gentleman did not speak although he seemed to understand what was said. Another young woman tried to speak, but her words were not decipherable. Mark seemed to tolerate the other "consumers" (the title given to the group home residents), but he was quite fond of a number of the staff and just loved to be with them. They seemed jovial and kind. It takes an exceptional person to work with adults with special needs.

When Mark first arrived at the home, he was fascinated with a bell that rang every time someone came in and out of the bathroom. He kept going in and out of the bathroom just so he could hear the bell. One of the guys at the group home got so mad at Mark that he went into the bathroom, yanked the bell off the wall and threw it out the front door!

Occasionally on my parent's visits, Mom brought fresh, homemade rolls for everyone. My parents felt good about Mark's care. If my mother was troubled about something, she shared her concern and it was addressed. My mother also wrote Mark once a week adding a recent family photograph and a little money. She was dedicated to her son, the last to leave home.

It took a number of years, but I knew my father had accepted Mark's move to the group home when he wrote the following letter after his eightieth birthday in December of 2005:

Dear Mark,

The Lord gave you to me knowing that I would take care of you as long as I could and would treat you like my other children. I have always loved you so very, very much.

When you left home it hurt me more than any child I had because I was afraid someone would abuse you and I would never stand for that. But the place you where you live now and love so much seems to be a caring home.

Mark, there will always be a soft spot in my heart for you, a spot that will never go away.

All my love, Dad

Research indicates that parents play an active role even after their child with Down syndrome moves to another residential environment. They have frequent contact with their child, maintaining strong and warm bonds of affection.

Dorothy Robison, Marty Wyngaarden Krauss, Marsha Mailick Seltzer, "Does Parenting Ever End?." Accessed at the National Down Syndrome Society (NDSS) website: www.ndss.org on January 15, 2004.
Reprinted with permission

Mark is standing in front of the group home where he happily lived for five years.

Mark's emotional attachment to his father is clearly revealed in this photograph.

People with Down syndrome need interaction with family, friends, peers, and others, just as other people do.

Dennis McGuire, Ph.D. & Brian Chicoine, M.D., Mental Wellness in Adults With Down Syndrome, (Bethesda, MD: Woodbine House, 2006).
Reprinted with permission

T-h-hank You

One of the wisest things my parents did while raising a son with Down syndrome in a large family was to enforce clear behavior standards for him. No, they didn't expect him to be able to read or write, but he had simple chores and if he misbehaved, he was punished. Unfortunately Dad's method was corporal punishment. So Mark was spanked like the rest of us if he did something wrong. I never remember him getting spankings as often as the rest of his siblings, but he grew up clearly knowing right from wrong. This made Mark well disciplined. Even the group home administrators had commented on Mark's habitual sweeping the floors, setting the table, and taking care of his personal hygiene. He also was a grateful man. Every time someone gave him a gift or performed a favor, he always said, "I appreciate that." I suppose that is why I loved to do special things for him. He did not say much, but his eyes and face just lit up.

In 2002, Mark was getting ready to turn fifty. A party was in order. He was already living in the group home, so we invited the entire group home plus all of our relatives and friends of the family to a party at my parent's church. We decorated with the theme of Mark's favorite things, sunshine and fishing. With bright yellow hanging sun decorations and hanging paper fish, the church assembly hall looked festive indeed. My daughter, Christin, and I carried LIVE goldfish all the way from a pet store in Durham, North Carolina (a detour we took after our arrival at the Raleigh airport), just to have as table decorations. My mother helped with the cake and food. We had a special large chair gaily adorned with balloons where the birthday boy would sit and be honored. We hired a bluegrass band to add to the festivities as Mark loved to dance.

In my parent's little town, a party is a big deal. Since it was Sunday we had the gathering in the late afternoon so that all the people who had evening commitments at their church could attend. It was wonderful to see family members and friends I had not seen for years. They all loved Mark and my parents, so the party was well attended. In addition we had invited the group home residents who seemed genuinely happy to be there.

When Mark walked in the door, I placed a party hat on his head and everyone cheered and clapped. You would have thought he was a politician. Instead of sitting down, he went around to each and every guest and either shook hands or delivered a big hug. He was clearly excited and so happy to see all of the familiar faces.

The food was good old down home cooking with chicken, potato salad, green beans, assorted vegetables, and desserts. The most popular items were Mom's rolls. The entire Gretna community loved my mother's homemade rolls. She made dozens and dozens each week as gifts and to be used to sell at charity events. Mark loved the food, but he was so excited he didn't seem to eat as much as usual.

It didn't take long until we had Mark up and dancing. He could step out with the best of 'em and actually had a good beat to the music. It was a delight to see him kick up his heels and try to copy the steps of fellow dancers. My brother Ken's children performed one of their school talent show comic acts as Mark looked on.

I had gotten up in front of the microphone several times to thank everyone for coming and begin the singing of "Happy Birthday." In the midst of the jollity I had not noticed that out of the blue Mark was at the microphone. He wanted to speak too.

"Oh, Lord, this could be dangerous," I told my sister as I held my breath. I wanted to rush up to the microphone and take it away, but something told me to wait.

A hush came over the crowd. No one could believe that Mark, this man whom they had accepted with all of his handicaps, had walked to the microphone unsolicited and was standing before us to speak.

He paused and looked around the room trying to make eye contact with each and everyone of us. "Thhank you," he softly spoke in the most heartfelt voice I had ever heard.

He said it again, "Thhank you." He continued to speak for several minutes with tears in his eyes. Whatever he said we could not understand, but we could feel the sincerity. He was clearly moved and so was everyone at the party.

It was a magical moment. It was a moment worth all the effort, time, and money spent to put this celebration together.

Mark, however, broke the magic when he started his ranting, "Pretttty in the morning, Prettty in the morning." He stridently said this as he made a motion like he was shaving.

Mark's time at the microphone was over as I discreetly grasped it from his hands, thanked him, and led him to the birthday chair to open gifts.

It is said that you should do something for someone who can never repay you. I thought I was doing just such a good deed this day for my brother. The fact is, he did something for ME far more than I could ever repay. He gave me the memory of grateful tears and "thhannk you." A priceless gift.

The estimated life expectancy of a person with Down syndrome is approximately twenty years less than the life expectancy for the general population. Therefore, the physical age of individuals with Down syndrome who are 40 to 50 years of age may be equivalent to individuals in the general population who are chronologically 60 to 70 years of age.

Brian Chicoine, MD, Dennis McGuire, PhD, Stephen Rubin, PhD, "Adults with Down Syndrome: Specialty Clinic Perspectives." Accessed online at www.ds-health.com/adults.htm, March 3, 2003. Reprinted with permission

An important social issue involves keeping the individual with Down syndrome as much involved in activities as possible. Keeping the adult involved in activities reflects the goal of maximizing function by stimulating the person at a level that is challenging but not overwhelming.

Brian Chicoine, MD, Dennis McGuire, PhD, Stephen Rubin, PhD, "Adults with Down Syndrome: Specialty Clinic Perspectives." Accessed online at www.ds-health.com/adults.htm, March 3, 2003. Reprinted with permission

It's About Time

Life at the group home was an adjustment, but the change benefited both Mark and our family. We saw Mark smiling, happy each time we visited. He still had that rascal smirk that we all loved to see. At first, he would not leave the home to go with anyone from the family, not even to get a hamburger at McDonalds®. He was afraid that we would take him back to my parents. Staff members explained to us that we had to be patient. Mark enjoyed my parent's weekly visits, but at first he would not even go to the door to say goodbye. His fear of being forced to go home was always present.

Gradually, however, Mark visited for brief periods, but always chose to return to the group home. He spent the night a few times, but we could tell the tension was there.

We knew how much he loved his family. When a family member came through the door of the group home, Mark beamed, jumped up, and bestowed a big hug on the lucky recipient. The staff revealed that although Mark loved being there, he also loved his family and needed that connection.

The key it seemed to me was a strong, supportive coordination and communication between the family and the staff who worked with Mark. Most people with special needs do not like change, and it affects their behavior. For example, once a new staff member was supposed to drive Mark home to visit for a few days. The staff member phoned and said, "Mark doesn't seem to want to come to your home. He is sitting on the floor and won't budge, and we can't force him."

"That's ok, we understand," my mother said calmly. When she spoke with me afterward, she said, "You know, I think Mark wasn't confident that this new staff member would return him to the group home. He has to have that trust."

Mark liked so many of the employees at the group home and day support. He teased with them and appeared to enjoy their company. I sensed a genuine spirit of caring each time I visited my brother. One of his favorite staff members recounted a humorous story about Mark and his love of money.

It seems that my brother was sitting next her when he asked, "Will you marry me?"

Knowing my brother quite well, this sensitive caregiver replied, "Well, yes, Mark, I will marry you, BUT I need a ring. You've got to get your money out of that wallet and go buy me a ring."

Mark looked over at her and then he pulled out his wallet which was attached to his belt by a massive silver chain. Carefully eyeing the enclosed dollar bills, he seemed to be mulling over the situation. He then looked at his friend's hand and stared back at his money. You could tell he was in a tight spot, what was he to do?

Finally he slowly turned to her and said, "Never mind."

During the first year, Mark traveled with the group to his first camp overnight. We had not allowed Mark to stay overnight at camp in Nashville for fear he might walk away. I was anxious to see how he would fare for an entire week. Apparently he did fine until two nights before the camp ended. That evening Mark was told that swimming time was over and he needed to get out of the pool. True to past behavior, Mark decided he did not care for this rule. In the middle of the night my brother decided he would go swimming. I'm sure the staff was traumatized when they couldn't find Mark anywhere, and in more distress when they discovered him in the POOL ALONE!

The director told my brother that he would have to leave. Mark would be the first "consumer" at the group home to be kicked out of camp! One of his favorite staff members came to get him. Upon arrival the group home employee was surprised to find that Mark had climbed way up in top of a very lofty tree. He was loudly "cussing out" the entire camp. She looked up into the tree and asked, "Mark, what in the world are you doing in that tree? Come on down, let's go home."

Mark looked down and smiled, so thrilled to see his friend. "It's about time," he stated matter-of-factly, and promptly climbed down the tree and went straight to the car.

We believe that he had had enough of camp and once more was afraid that he would not see his new home again. He also enjoyed the routine of his daily activities at the support center where he ate lunch, went on short excursions, and watched television or worked with crafts in the afternoon.

I suppose if Mark could tell all of us, he would say that it took a long time for us to understand that he needed to live in a place where he was happy and could be treated as much as possible as an adult. I'm positive he would say, "It's about time!"

The tension between the need for family and the desire to break away reflect the continuing redefinition of the parent-child relationship that occurs throughout the life of a child. Ideally, this relationship results in increasing independence for the child, while emotional bonds and positive social influences are maintained. Finding this balance results in the development of a sense of self and independence by the young person, and the continuing support and encouragement of his family.

Cheryl Hanley-Maxwell, "Families: The Heart of Transition." Accessed at the National Down Syndrome Society (NDSS) website: www.ndss.org on July 12, 2004.
Reprinted with permission

In a longitudinal study, differences and similarities between brothers and sisters of adults with mental retardation with respect to the instrumental (caregiving, companionship) and affective (positive affect, emotion) aspects of the sibling relationship were examined. Sisters scored high in the caregiving, companionship, and positive affect aspects of the sibling relationship.

Gael J. Orsmond and Marsha Mailick Seltzer, "Brothers and Sisters of Adults with Mental Retardation: Gendered Nature of the Sibling Relationship," *American Journal on Mental Retardation*, 2000, Vol. 105, No. 6, pp 486-508.

You're My Sister

Anyone coming out of anesthesia can envision many things—perhaps a loved one in a dreamy state of unfocused images. When Mark came out of anesthesia after his pacemaker was implanted, he must have seen golden arches. The first words out of his mouth to my mother and sister were, "Going to McDonalds." You just have to smile.

Mark had been having occasional fainting spells since the 1990s and they were becoming more frequent. The doctors could not get his heart rate steady. Mark had fainted once when he visited in Nashville, but I had attributed it to running during the summer heat. Apparently these spells were more serious than we or his caregivers had thought. It made me rest easy knowing that the pacemaker implantation in 2003 seemed to have solved the fainting problem.

That was just one issue. As the aging process gives rise to required adjustments as our body machines break down, an adult with Down syndrome has even more problems that seem to multiply with age. Of course, because they do age ten to twenty years faster than their peers, Mark was more like a seventy-two-year-old rather than a fifty-two-year-old when his pacemaker was installed.

Mark's health had been remarkably good considering his age and genetic condition. Adults with Down syndrome manifest a number of physical conditions that can be serious and require extra monitoring. Physical exercise and Mark's love of swimming and basketball helped to keep him in great shape. With the onset of fainting spells there was a concern with his health, so Mark was taken to the doctor. While in the office Mark fainted again and was immediately admitted to the hospital. Tests revealed an irregular heart rate. In ICU (intensive care) they could not get it to stabilize, which led to the decision to implant the pacemaker.

The simple surgery went well, but when Mark came out of anesthesia, strangers were wheeling him back to his room. Not understanding what had just happened he panicked and tried to escape from the moving gurney. It required five hospital members to hold him in place until they were able to restrain him with straps to his bed. Not knowing how to work with him, the staff told Mark it was important to be still. That information was meaningless, he could not comprehend what they were trying to explain. In came our sister, Dianna. Immediately upon seeing her, my brother relaxed.

Knowing just the thing to calm Mark, she said, "If you settle down, I will take you to McDonalds and buy you a cup of hot coffee."

Whoa! Hot coffee, McDonalds! He looked at her as if he had just heard his favorite song on the radio! He became calm and smiled.

In order for the pacemaker to stay in place, Mark's arm had to be restrained for six weeks. This would require close monitoring. Already the hospital staff was having difficulty keeping his arm in place. Again, my astute sister suggested that they bandage his arm.

"I know it isn't necessary, but he will connect the bandage to immobility and therefore conform to your request," Dianna calmly suggested. "Plus he will love the attention of what he perceives as a broken arm."

The staff took the recommendation and voila, Mark was very careful with his arm! A little understanding of these special folks goes a long way.

My sister frequently visited Mark after her day of teaching. Occasionally she took him to dinner or just dropped by the group home. Each time, he embraced her grinning ear to ear, and said, "You're my sister."

She took time to speak with the staff to see how his week had gone. They kept a detailed journal of Mark's daily activities, including his sleep patterns. Between my parents and sister's visits and the care given by the group home staff, Mark had a cadre of interested caregivers wanting the best for our brother.

Although living at the group home was his first choice, there were times after the initial move (albeit rare) when my brother became lonely. Mom and Dad visited during the day, but there were evenings when Mark felt the desire to get in touch with his relatives. He needed little more than to hear our voices or see someone from the family to lift his spirits. At these times a staff member from the group home called to advise us of this need.

When anyone had trouble with Mark, however, no one could better handle him than my sister. Mark somehow connected with Dianna. Although she had rules and made him obey, it was clear she loved him. Perhaps he sensed that Dianna knew him better than anyone.

Dianna was the one sibling physically close enough to attend the regular group home meetings, and my parents liked having her there. With my father's hearing loss and my mother sometimes misunderstanding what was being conveyed, Dianna became an invaluable part of the sessions. As an educator she was more familiar with some of the medical terminology and behavioral issues.

Between 2003 and 2006, there have been numerous changes at the group home. The house was completely remodeled in the spring of 2003 and all of the "consumers" had to stay at a motel for a week while the work was being completed. Shortly after moving back into the house, there was also personnel turnover which included one of Mark's favorite staff members. These changes were difficult for Mark. We felt it triggered depression, and reflected in my brother's behavior. At times the personnel were challenged with Mark when he wouldn't conform to the rules of the day-support center and his residential home. He only obeyed if they promised to take him to his beloved McDonalds.

This struck a chord with Dianna, "Well, guys, Mark is using you because you are rewarding him for bad behavior. Let me speak with him."

Dianna dropped by to see Mark right before his doctor's appointment. She spent at least thirty minutes talking to him. Dianna knew he was listening, but he tried the same trick with her.

"McDonalds, go to McDonalds," he responded.

"Mark, you know I usually take you to McDonalds, but because of your inappropriate behavior, I will NOT take you there today," she calmly said.

"McDonalds," he repeated.

After discussing his unacceptable behavior, Dianna said that if he would act properly, she would drive him there next week but NOT today.

Mark understood, but was mad. Usually he hugged her and said, "You're my sister."

That day, no hug. As Mark was walking Dianna to the door, she met a new staff member.

"Who is this, Mark?" asked the caregiver.

Instead of his usual introduction, "This is my sister,"

Mark said only, "Dianna." My sister knew he was angry.

"Remember, I'll take you to McDonald's next time, if you have been good," she repeated.

Mark, who can't seem to stay mad at Dianna for long, held her close as she walked out the door. As she left, he yelled from the house, "YOU'RE MY SISTER!"

Dianna had become more than Mark's sister. With my parents almost eighty years old, she accepted their request to become my brother's Legally Authorized Representative (LAR). In this capacity Dianna acted on behalf of Mark. When appointing a LAR, the community services agency considers the consumer's wishes as much as possible. I had no doubt that Mark would select Dianna to speak for him. She had been the family member phoned when the staff had trouble with Mark or when they needed to convey information. It was only natural that she would assume this responsibility. After submitting paperwork, Dianna officially became Mark's representative in 2005. She made major decisions with regard to my brother in consultation with his case worker and group home staff. So that she did not have to bear all the burden, Dianna occasionally called me for consultation and support. She also had input on Mark's status from my parent's weekly visitations. I became the communicator of "Mark updates" for the extended family, with my sister being the "on-site" guardian.

Dianna's approach with Mark somehow worked. When no one could get him to behave, with only one look from my sister, Mark responded! After one particular meeting, he refused to get in the van to go home. A staff member shared the problem with my sister explaining that she did not think Mark really understood.

"Oh, yes he does!" my sister stated emphatically. "Watch this."

Dianna walked calmly outside. Mark took one look

at her and said, "I'm sorry," and immediately hopped into the van.

The staff member told Dianna that she wouldn't have believed it had she not seen this immediate compliance with my sister's mere presence.

There have been times when Mark didn't obey anyone, not even Dianna, but those were rare. Dianna had patience, love, and a nurturing spirit with which Mark had connected and responded to since he was a little boy. He hadn't forgotten all those years.

I have been so grateful for my sister's willingness to step up and take responsibility for being Mark's legal representative. She spoke on behalf of my parents and us siblings, taking an interest for Mark's welfare, doing so willingly and with no regrets. Times could be tough, especially the times when Mark had to be hospitalized. My husband, Clark, wrote Dianna after a particularly challenging time. His email reflects the family's sentiments:

Dear Dianna,

I have been meaning to tell you something... and never seem to find the right time or place, or method. THANKS for being my sister-in-law, and for your goodness to Mark and so many others. You are one of God's many "earth-angels" who just seems to always be flying around the right place doing His will for those who can't do it for themselves.

You give so much, offer so much, and are just one of those "get out of my way" people who find obstacles and remove them when it comes to doing what you feel is right.

The Lord will richly reward your goodness, and Mark is so very blessed to have you. I have had him on my mind much of these days, seeing that little impish smile and those big hugs. I feel that these little set-backs, although they are a progression, are just ways of preparing us for that which all of us will face one day, that of "going home."

He's not ready yet, nor are any of us, but he is slipping away each day, not from this recent situation, the old body is just not what it was.

It seems just like yesterday when he'd come visit that he could run around the lake and get so far ahead of me, that I could not even keep up. And now he's slow, a bit fumbly, and just like the rest of us,
slowing down a bit. While I see it in myself in small ways, I know that our life is not our own, and we could go any day in any way.

All of this to say, thank you for doing all you do, and I know its not always fun or what you might like to be doing. I can't believe you even had your vacation taken away, but then again, that is just like you.
God bless you my friend, thanks for being there.
Clark

Dianna's added responsibility of being Mark's legal representative was daunting. Being conscientious, she would forego her own desires and wellbeing just to help my brother.

Just like Mark, I myself am proud to say, "You're my sister."

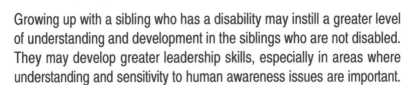

Growing up with a sibling who has a disability may instill a greater level of understanding and development in the siblings who are not disabled. They may develop greater leadership skills, especially in areas where understanding and sensitivity to human awareness issues are important.

Rick Berkobien, "Siblings: Brothers and Sisters of People Who Have Mental Retardation." Copyright 1995-2003, accessed on line at The Arc, http://www.nas.com/downsyn/siblings.html on July 12, 2004.
Reprinted with permission

Joining a local religious community can be a real boon for people with disabilities...many congregations welcome people with disabilities and would be interested in helping them resolve problems...

Linda J. Stengle, M.H.S.. "How Do I Help Develop Relationships for My Child?", Laying Community Foundations for Your Child with a Disability, (Bethesda,: Woodbine House, 1996). pg. 55. Reprinted with permission

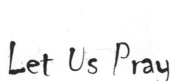

Let Us Pray

Angel of God
My guardian dear
To whom God's love entrusts me near
Ever this day be at my side
To light, to guard, to rule, to guide
Amen

Each morning I have always recited this prayer several times—one for my brother, one for my family, and one especially for Mark's caregivers. Being such a distance away helped me to entrust Mark's care to God, who is ultimately in charge of all of us.

Scholars are currently researching the daunting question, "Does prayer help heal?" Those of us who believe in the power of prayer have no doubt. I've decided that if God wishes for someone to come "home," no amount of prayer will change that, but I also believe that prayer has helped to heal. There are circumstances in our lives that to non-believers would seem circumstantial, but I call them Providential. I've seen it in Mark's life many times:

—The mere decision to NOT take the physician's advice and put Mark in an institution was guided by my parent's faith. They firmly believed that God would help them with this special child.

—Just surviving that first year of life seemed miraculous. Mark could not have been more than a few weeks old when he was admitted to the hospital with the diagnosis of double pneumonia. The doctor said, "I fear your child will not make it through the night. I'm sorry." Upon hearing this sobering news my mother's sister rushed to the hospital. My Aunt Catherine's strong belief in God included leading her family of nine children in a nightly recitation of the rosary (a Catholic devotional litany of prayers). When she arrived at Mark's bedside my aunt opened a small bottle of Lourdes water. People from all over the world travel to Lourdes, France, to pray and carry away the healing water from the famous city. It was at Lourdes that the Virgin Mary appeared to a young girl named Bernadette. Numerous miracles of healing have been documented there and the water is said to have a powerful healing energy. "I believe this might help baby Mark," she thought. My aunt poured a small amount of the holy water onto her hand and gently patted it on Mark's tiny leg. She stood before this ill child praying that a miracle might occur.

The next morning Mark looked more active, not as pale.

"I can't believe this," the doctor declared. "The pneumonia appears to have vanished! This baby is going to live."

—When Dianna and I were looking for a satisfactory group home for Mark one option initially appealing to us was a place that housed a small number of residents. It seemed to offer each individual one-on-one attention and the farm like setting was similar to my brother's family life. There was a delay, however, which led us to select the group home where he happily resided for many years. Just recently the manager of the earlier option was in the newspaper citing possible abuse allegations and the residential home is no longer in business. We were led the right direction.

——In later years, Mark had a fainting episode in front of the cardiologist when he was brought in for a routine exam. Immediately the physician sent my brother to the hospital only to discover that a wire had come loose in his pacemaker. Had the loose wire remained undetected, Mark's health would have been in jeopardy.

My mother is a role model for all of her children. We admiringly refer to her as "Saint Ruth." Her giving spirit, selfless actions, and profound faith have been at the core of our family spirit. Because her own mother died when she was only sixteen one might think that this might have challenged her love of God; instead it deepened her faith. My father converted to Catholicism when they married but never caught the fervor my mother had until later in life. Dad is now known for his grace before meals. He will not begin until everyone is paying close attention, then he carefully, fervently, and very slowly leads us in prayer.

St. Francis once said, "Preach the Gospel at all times, if necessary use words." I saw the gospel revealed to me through my mother's actions. It was Mom who made all seven of us get up every Sunday and march dutifully to Mass. Just getting to church was a challenge. Mark would have to be dressed, and there always seemed to be a missing shoe or something that would make us late. BUT we were there, some of us half asleep, taking up an entire pew. That persistence and example helped form my belief system which I treasure to this day. I owe a debt of gratitude to my mother for planting and nurturing that seed of faith.

In the church we have seven sacraments. Most dutiful Catholic parents make certain their children are baptized, make their first penance, receive their first holy communion, and last but not least are confirmed. Mark was treated no differently than the rest of us. He received all of these sacraments (with the exception of confirmation).

The sacrament of Penance, however, was abandoned after a few sessions. In this sacrament, one confesses his or her sins to a priest and is absolved of them with a few prayers usually added as a penance for wrongdoings. Mother would advise the priest that her son with Down syndrome would be confessing next and it might be difficult to understand him. Mark entered the small room which was about the size of a closet and quite dark. Mom had left the door slightly cracked open so that my brother would not be afraid. From the stillness of the church we were shocked to hear Mark go into a tirade telling the priest what all his BROTHERS AND SISTERS had done wrong! Mark did not realize that he was supposed to tell only HIS sins. The last time in the confessional box resulted in him fainting and falling out of the tiny room. We can only assume that he was too hot or nervous. The priest assured my mother that Mark already had a place in heaven and confession was no longer a necessity.

The ritual of attending Mass for so many years appears to have created a soft spot in Mark's heart. When he entered the church he was always quiet and never mumbled. He remembered the way he was taught to act in this place of worship. While his caregivers were unable to take him to Sunday Mass, when Mark visited on holidays he always attended with us. At times I glanced at my brother and he had tears in his eyes. Did he feel the serenity in this holy place? Was this a reminder of times gone by, causing him to be sentimental? Whatever the reason, Mark captured the essence of the meaning behind going to church, perhaps even more than the regular churchgoers. He just seemed to understand.

Maybe Mark knew where to turn for help more than we realized. At one bi-annual meeting regarding my brother's stay at the group home the entire room of nine people discussed his well-being. He sat there in front of his case worker, my mother, sister, niece, group home and day-staff caregivers sound asleep, occasionally waking up only to nod off again. Dianna was making a strong point about Mark being overmedicated. An intense discussion ensued concerning this matter when suddenly something triggered Mark to awaken. Shocking everyone, he blurted out, "LET US PRAY!" With his head bowed and his hands folded there came an outpouring of unintelligible garble which no one could understand except they knew Mark was deep in prayer.

Dianna said, "You know maybe Mark is trying to tell us something here." This certainly calmed the discussion, and the meeting ended in a peaceful manner in which all agreed they would work toward improving Mark's situation.

Prayer along with a strong faith were saving graces for Mark.

Approximately 7 out of 10 children with Down syndrome pray on a regular basis.

Cynthia S. Kidder and Brian Skotko, "Band of Angels Press Survey" in *Common Threads, Celebrating Life with Down Syndrome*, Rochester Hills: Band of Angels Press, 2001, pg. 2. Reprinted with permission

This photograph was taken of Mark on the day of his First Holy Communion. The sacred sacrament is memorable in the lives of most Catholics.

When included in your child's network, siblings can provide a continuity that you would be hard pressed to find anywhere else in life today. A motivated sibling can make a very positive impact on the life of a person with a disability.

Linda J. Stengle, MHS, "How Do I Help Develop Relationships for My Child?" Laying Community Foundations for Your Child with a Disability, (Bethesda: Woodbine House, 1996), pg. 85. Reprinted with permission

Hey, I Wanna Tell You Something

The Houston sun was unrelenting the morning I flew to Virginia in July 2005. I was halfway happy to have a break from the continuous heat. We were in dire need of rain with no relief in sight, yet the heavy humidity stifled the city. It was miserable to be outside.

Dianna had phoned that the group home was having some behavioral problems with Mark. He was not getting in the van when asked, he was staying up all night and would not wear the CPAP (Continuous Positive Airway Pressure) apparatus that was considered to be the best treatment for his sleep apnea.

His alertness seemed to fluctuate drastically. One day when my parents visited Mark would be attentive and excited to see them, the next time, he was sleeping and could barely talk. When asked about Mark's lethargy, the staff attributed it to lack of sleep. Dianna had observed similar instability. "I'm going to bring him to my house for three days for observation and to see if he has regressed," she said. "If you want, I'd love for you to be here."

Her fear was that the staff was going to increase behavior medication, making him a zombie. We didn't want that quality of life for him. We had seen Mark like this before when his behavior was being chemically controlled. It was pathetic to see the once bright eyes glazed over, having to be led every step by a staff member. His once quirky fun personality had vanished.

With much persuasion and his doctor's insistence, Mark was weaned off behavioral medications. After this accomplishment and with the cooperation of the staff, the "old Mark had returned." The behavior meds were then limited to an inconsequential dose at night to help him sleep. He could walk without help, he was speaking more clearly. We were encouraged. Without drugs he was more active. The positive behaviors returned, as well as the negative. On a positive note, he was fun and witty. He loved going places, eating out, dancing, and teasing. On the negative side, he regressed to the familiar stubbornness and the demanding repetitions such as "McDonalds, McDonalds, McDonalds."

This was not harmful behavior in itself, but if staff was out with six or seven other people with special needs it became a major problem.

Mark decided he didn't want to get on the van one afternoon and kept people stranded for almost two hours while they worked diligently to coax him back into the vehicle. The director had to drive out and deal with the situation. In the end he was sweet-talked into the bus with a mere cup of coffee.

We disagreed with several staff about Marks's behavior. Some staff believed this was something Mark couldn't control and medication did the trick. We believed that Mark could control certain aspects and that behavior modification would be a better answer than a medication prescribed for schizophrenic behavior which made him seem to be in a trance.

I remember one well-meaning caregiver said, "I think your family wants Mark to be like he was years ago. He's not. Aging has affected his health."

"This could be true," I agreed. "But the drug is simply making him lethargic—what kind of quality is that? We don't disagree with using medication if it helps, we just want to try something that would not take away the essence of his personality."

These words ran through my mind as I landed in Raleigh, North Carolina (the closest airport city to Gretna) where Dianna was there to greet me and drive the two hour journey to Gretna. We chatted all the way home and planned our activities for Mark.

The next morning as we drove down her tree-lined drive to pick up Mark, the harbinger of a good trip befell us as we spotted a doe sauntering across the road. Dianna slowed down and said, "Mom told me that if there is one deer, be cautious, there would be more." We didn't expect to see a baby fawn gingerly totter out in front of the car. He stood there on little scrawny legs which held up the beautiful tiny spotted body and perfectly formed head. He was amazing, causing us to ooh and aah inside the vehicle. "Darn, I wish I had my camera," Dianna said. I reflected upon Mark who was like this fawn; although now fifty-three years old, he was in a never ending "fawn" stage, still so fragile and innocent.

Arriving at the group home we found Mark quite chipper, singing "Happy Birthday" to himself. He was playful and giggly.

"I love this place," he proclaimed as he hugged us.

"He had a good night and is all set, ready to go," the house manager said.

"You want to go swimming, Mark?" Dianna asked.

"I stay here," he replied, enjoying the extra attention he was receiving with all the residents away at the day support center.

"Well, how about McDonalds? You want to go to McDonalds?" we asked.

McDonalds was irresistible! With packed bag we headed for the golden arches. Dianna knew the routine:

"Take him in, order the Number 1 with no onions and add a diet drink. He likes to fill the cup himself."

Exactly as she predicted, He sat down to the Big Mac, fries, and a Coke. Very slowly he ate his lunch with much satisfaction.

Dianna and I sat discussing the agenda for the day. "Hey, there's a new shoe outlet in Gretna. Let's check it out on our way home," she suggested.

"Fine with me," I said, curious about the store myself.

Feeling sufficiently stuffed, Mark followed us into the outlet. Only two customers were milling around. Dianna and I browsed the racks noting that the shoes were well made but weren't particularly bargain priced. Meanwhile, Mark had seen the bathroom symbol.

"Dianna, should I let him?" I asked. Mark's fetish for bathrooms where he might stay for hours made me hesitate.

"Well, ok, "she said, "but Mark, don't be long."

Ten minutes passed.

"Mark," I said, quietly knocking on the door. "Let's go. We're ready to leave."

No response.

I put my ear next to the door. I could hear the toilet paper roll moving. By the sound of things he must have used a plethora of tissue, and it would be in the toilet! I could visualize a nightmare of the commode overflowing onto the floor, out the door, into the store, ruining the new carpet, and creating chaos in an otherwise sleepy town. Heck, this could prompt someone to "call the sheriff" just to give the police a little action!

Dianna joined me. "Mark, I said open this door!" she called to him.

No response. The store employees were becoming agitated. You could see the irritation in their glances!

"Mark, please unlock this door, we must leave or no coffee for you!" said Dianna.

She heard the familiar roll of the toilet paper. Then a

flush. I held my breath hoping not to see water trickling underneath the door.

Dianna sought out a clerk, asking for a key. The store had recently been opened, and appeared to have no key for the bathroom. The clerk called for backup. More keys were brought from another building but none worked.

My sister decided to take matters in her own hands. She took out her OWN keys. This was a simple lock, it couldn't be that much trouble. Sure enough, she was able to jiggle the lock and open the door.

No sooner had she opened the door, than Mark turned away from the toilet.

"I'm sorry," he said. She grabbed his arm leading him toward the door. I stayed behind to assess the damage. The toilet had not overflowed, but a huge wad of tissue was sitting there, a silent threat inside the bowl. I quickly disposed of the gob of tissue, grateful it had not stopped up the thing!

We apologized and headed home. There seemed to be little understanding from the clerks for our frustrations and it seemed fruitless to even try to explain our situation.

I lost it with Mark. To show my displeasure, I emptied his McDonald's drink on the ground. "You were bad Mark, no Coke!" I exclaimed.

My sister looked at me in dismay, and I realized that anger was the wrong way to deal with Mark. It really didn't solve the problem.

At home things settled down. We tried to explain to Mark that he can't stay holed up in the bathroom, particularly in a public place. No more would we allow him to go into a bathroom with a lock unless we were in the room.

The afternoon brought a delightful swimming time. Mark had not been swimming since he jumped into the public pool in his underwear. We weren't sure how he would do being heavier. Mark had gained thirty pounds in the group home from too much food and not enough exercise, which were his choices.

At first he slowly went into the pool, but it wasn't long before he was swimming freestyle. He remembered! He did not have the same stamina of years gone by, but he still could swim! We gave him a float and he paddled around on that, enjoying the water again after an extended absence.

Mark went to bed that night tired but content.

The next day he awoke noticeably more tired and disoriented. He had not worn the CPAP as this was a new machine, one Dianna had not seen before and she had not been sure how to connect it.

My brother seemed markedly less "with it" and not as coherent. He wasn't even sure of our names.

The next evening after Dianna called to get proper instructions on how to use the new machine, we made sure he wore the CPAP. She told me that the new apparatus had an added oxygen component. The sleep specialist had prescribed the added oxygen since it was determined that Mark was only getting sixty percent oxygen when he slept. Dianna was uncomfortable with bringing the oxygen machine. She wasn't sure how to attach it, plus it was large and cumbersome. She felt he would be fine for a few days without the oxygen component.

She was wrong.

By the third morning Mark was even more sluggish and fell asleep sitting in a chair. His breathing was labored. It was clear the doctor was correct. The effect on Mark without the added oxygen appeared to have made a drastic change in his daily life. Dianna recalled the doctor had said that this could be a life-threatening situation if the sleep apnea continued without treatment! Mark's ankles were also swollen indicating poor circulation. The doctor had explained that when he slept one side of the heart was working so hard to get that oxygen; it was enlarging, causing heart problems.

We took Mark to the lake to enjoy time with my parents, fishing on their pontoon boat. It was a hot day but the canopy on the pontoon would provide enough shade. We were pleased that Mark had remembered how to cast out his fishing rod. He had to have a little help but he was obviously happy to be on the lake. Shortly, however, I saw Mark sitting up, pole in hand, sleeping. This was one of his favorite pastimes and he was too tired to enjoy it!

By the time we packed his bags and brought him back to the group home it was clear to us that the sleep apnea was taking its toll on Mark and his quality of life.

Dianna and I were shocked at the difference in Mark between using the CPAP plus oxygen and skipping it. Each day without it brought a more somnolent brother. The very next day Dianna conferred with Mark's doctor and he was adamant. Mark must wear the CPAP with oxygen every night. This was no longer a choice for Mark, but because it was life threatening it was now mandatory.

Mark used to walk up to us and say, "Hey, I wanna tell you something." He would proceed to explain some story to us. Because we had a difficult time understanding him, we could only dechiper a few words here and there. Now, by his extreme fatigue he was crying out, "Hey, I wanna tell you something. I need help cause my choice to stay up late and not wear the CPAP is not working, it's ruining my health!"

I flew back enlightened, seeing clearly the problem was not medication but sleep apnea and praying that the group home would agree and work with us for Mark's benefit. He needed to wear the CPAP with oxygen every night. The challenge for the staff would be to help Mark go to bed at a reasonable hour and persuade him to wear the CPAP.

Upon reflection, I realize that Mark wanted to tell ALL of us something and if he could have articulated his feelings to us and to his caregivers here is what I think he would have said:

1. Don't overmedicate me—I know I'm easier to handle, but being a zombie and taking away my personality is not how I want to live!
2. I love that the group home gives me choices, but give me two healthy choices rather than allow me so much freedom. I am not mature mentally so I sometimes make choices like a five-year-old would make.
3. Be patient with me. I am a good person but I'm stubborn.
4. I love my caregivers, and I want all of them to help me and love me.
5. I love my family's visits. I don't want to go back home to live, but I love seeing them.
6. Just like most people, there are certain individuals I like and certain people with whom I am not comfortable and I will respond accordingly.
7. When I can't be understood, it's frustrating. Walk in my shoes one day and you'll see.
8. Give me responsibilities that I can handle. I want to have a job.
9. I love to get mail, especially from friends and family and ESPECIALLY if a dollar is enclosed.
10.   I love this place— moving me would destroy me.

Working with families whose children have disabilities is demanding work and takes a special commitment of not only time but also the willingness to open oneself to new ways of thinking and to reach beyond any barriers.

Lauren C. Berman, Linda Freeman, and David T. Helm, "People and Programs," in *Medical Care for Children & Adults with Developmental Disabilities - Second Edition*, eds.
J. Leslie Rubin, MD, Allen C. Crocker, MD, (Baltimore: Paul H. Brookes Publishing Co, 2006), pg. 43.

The Adult Down Syndrome Program in Atlanta provides specialty health services for individuals with Down syndrome in collaboration with ISDD (the Institute for the Study of Disadvantage and Disability) and the TEAM Centers, Inc.

ISDD (Institute for the Study or Disadvantage and Disability), TEAM Centers, Inc. (specialties in developmental disabilities), and DSAA (Down Syndrome Association of Atlanta), *Adult Down Syndrome Program (pamphlet)*. Assessible at www.isdd-home.org. Reprinted with permission

All That Traffic!

Nestled in the middle of a ritzy Atlanta neighborhood was a small nondescript house that became a spark of hope for my brother. After extensive research Dianna and I had found a center specifically designed to serve adults with Down syndrome. We were hoping that here we could find experts who would be familiar with the medical and behavioral issues of this special group and might have suggestions to help with Mark's medication and behavior issues.

The trek was not an easy one, but we were anxious to have Mark examined at the center. The plan was for me to fly from Houston to Greensboro, North Carolina. Dianna would stop by the group home and gather Mark, his luggage as well as his medical "cocktails" (his huge cadre of pills). The two would drive an hour and a half to the airport and wait for me at baggage claim. We would then drive four hours, spend the night in a hotel (which included bringing in the CPAP machine—the oxygen component made the machine awkward and cumbersome to transport), and finally reach our destination in Atlanta the next day.

As I came down the airport escalator Mark greeted me with a big hug and was happy to roll my bags to the car. Although he seemed somewhat unstable I let him take my luggage, holding onto his arm to help stabilize him. It was raining and it was rush hour. Dianna was not thrilled to be driving under these circumstances, but everything was going as planned.

We spent the night in a hotel, which Mark loves to do, but I was worried about his state of mind. He seemed in a fog. My sister informed me that supposedly Mark had had a "seizure." He cut his head and the staff called an ambulance. Without touching base with his primary physician, the emergency doctor had TRIPLED his dosage of anti-seizure medication. We were discouraged that again Mark was back to a zombie state. He also was visibly shaking. It was heartbreaking. This strengthened our resolve to find someone who could professionally help us!

Since Mark likes to spend A LOT of time in the bathroom, our stops had to be strategically planned. We had to take him with us to the women's restroom. The plan worked well. I went in first and scouted the room for ladies. If someone was there I waited until she left, rushed to the door, and motioned for Dianna to quickly bring Mark into a stall. Dianna urged Mark to do his "business," hushing him if he started to speak. It was interesting to see the expressions on people's faces if they heard a man's voice in the bathroom. As soon as the coast was clear, I helped Dianna hustle our hostage out the door and into the car. Mark walked like an old man and had to be prodded along. After the third time of sneaking into bathrooms Mark giggled. He kind of liked this new game, but the whole process was an ordeal for my sister and me.

The center we were consulting was an obscure house situated in a lovely Peachtree residential area. We were told later that the team liked a warmer atmosphere of a home and not a sterile clinic. I was a little skeptical initially, walking into the aged traditional-style house that might have been constructed in the 1950s. The carpet and furniture were obviously worn, but art scattered throughout the center added an optimistic spirit. What lacked in the decor was made up by the staff. From the moment we opened the door, we were warmly greeted. To heck with decor, I thought, we just might find kindred spirits here.

After about an hour of speaking with the social worker and center director, we were to meet Dr. Leslie Rubin, a developmental physician. The first hour had been spent looking over medical records and getting a little background information on Mark.

"Oh my, you came all the way from Virginia, just to see me. I guess I've got to do a good job, don't I?" Dr. Rubin greeted us. He immediately charmed us with his rich accent. Although a native of South Africa, he has been in Atlanta for more than eleven years. His casual, caring manner made us comfortable. Mark sat there and for the most part slept through much of the interview.

Dianna and I figured two hours would be a good session. Let Dr. Rubin meet Mark, view his records, clearly see that he is overmedicated, give us a game plan for working with his primary physician, and we'd be on our way. I remember the conversation this way.

"Let's start at the beginning," he said. "When did you first see a change in Mark? When did behavior problems begin?"

My sister began sharing the group home struggles with Mark's behavior.

Dr. Rubin squirmed in his chair. "Well, yes, I see," he probed. "We'll get to that but let's go back. When did you see Mark initially having troubles?"

"Well, Dianna, you recall that we discussed Mark became restless after Dad and Mom sold the recreation center," I said.

Dianna agreed and described how happy Mark had been working at the recreation center and what a huge disappointment its sale was to him. She recalled that it was around that same time that our youngest brother, Chris, had graduated from high school and left for college. That, too, affected Mark.

We then began a long discussion of Mark growing up and the events in his life that probably affected him greatly. Dr. Rubin began to peel away the onion, trying to get at the core of Mark's behavior. It helped us to realize how profoundly the loss of the recreation center and the concurrent event of Chris leaving home affected Mark. Later at the group home, he also missed the friendship of one staff member who had known Mark for years and no longer worked there.

Dr. Rubin was extremely empathetic, confirming the difficult aspects of Mark's circumstances. He might say occasionally, "Oh, what a loss for him. How profound. Wow, what Shakespeare could have done with this tragedy!"

Then we reviewed the list of medications, beginning with one that severely limited Mark's functionality, then adding the myriad of drugs for numerous ailments prescribed by various doctors.

"Oh, my, this can be very complicated, very complicated," Dr. Rubin said, pacing the floor.

Mark awakened to the sound of his voice.

"Come, Mark, stand up I want to examine you. I really like that watch of yours," he calmly said. My brother seemed to respond. It was funny because he seemed to hear this gentle doctor although Dr. Rubin never raised his voice. In fact while the physician was taking off his shirt, Mark said, "Peek-a-boo!" Dr. Rubin laughed and responded back with a "Peek-a-boo."

After the examination, Dr. Rubin said he'd like to work with his physician in Danville via phone to help improve Mark's situation. Then he suggested a follow-up visit in the summer. He recommended that Mark have only one doctor prescribing his medications. He was going to talk with his primary physician, review his medications and perhaps reduce some. He also agreed to be a consultant if and when Mark's physician wanted his expertise.

The two-hour session we had planned expanded to four hours! We had totally lost track of time. The good doctor took a photo of the three of us, and we left with positive feelings. Could this be the answer we'd hoped for? Would we now have a resource with whom Mark's physician could consult and use for guidance to help our brother?

Just as we had begun the trip during rush hour, we were ending in the same manner. Atlanta traffic is horrendous! Had Mark been more alert he would have looked around and said, "All that traffic!" —a mantra he used to repeat in years gone by. But it didn't bother us. We were leaving for home having "peeled the onion" realizing possibilities for our brother. We had hopeful hearts.

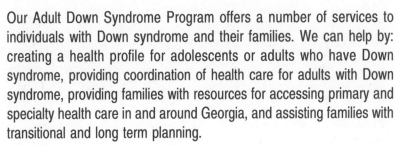

Our Adult Down Syndrome Program offers a number of services to individuals with Down syndrome and their families. We can help by: creating a health profile for adolescents or adults who have Down syndrome, providing coordination of health care for adults with Down syndrome, providing families with resources for accessing primary and specialty health care in and around Georgia, and assisting families with transitional and long term planning.

ISDD (Institute for the Study or Disadvantage and Disability), TEAM Centers, Inc. (specialties in developmental disabilities), and DSAA (Down Syndrome Association of Atlanta), *Adult Down Syndrome Program (pamphlet)*. Assessible at www.isdd-home.org. Reprinted with permission

Not a day went by without Mark checking the mail box at the group home. This photograph shows his excitement as he discovers there is mail and it's for him!

The healing words of a caring provider can reverberate throughout all aspects of a family's life. Guiding families in setting realistic goals, recognizing their children's strengths, supporting them in grieving their losses, and helping them to brainstorm creative solutions to difficult problems are central themes in this work.

Lauren C. Berman, Linda Freeman, and David T. Helm, "People and Programs," in *Medical Care for Children & Adults with Developmental Disabilities - Second Edition*, eds. I. Leslie Rubin, MD, Allen C. Crocker, MD, (Baltimore: Paul H. Brookes Publishing Co, 2006), pg. 55.

I Love This Place

The trip to Atlanta was fruitful. Dr. Rubin had several phone conversations with Mark's primary physician and was impressed with his knowledge of my brother and his medical status. In turn, Mark's physician seemed to welcome the expertise of a specialist in the area of Down syndrome. Now, if Mark's physician needed to consult with someone about Mark, he had the man!

Not long after our November 2005 trip, the cardiologist discovered that one of Mark's wires in the pacemaker had come loose and it had to be corrected. My sister and I felt the pacemaker disconnection, in addition to problems caused by his sleep apnea, was another reason Mark had been so lethargic. Mark went under anesthesia again and had a hospital stay. He did well and loved all the attention from the nurses, his family, and the group home staff.

Dr. Rubin's first suggestion was to have a behavioral specialist work with Mark and the group staff to persuade my brother to wear his sleep apparatus (CPAP) nightly. His physician concurred and called for a meeting with my sister and a caregiver from the group home. For his health to improve, Mark's physician was keenly aware of the importance of wearing the CPAP nightly. Before the meeting called in February, 2006, the good doctor had gently prodded the staff about wearing the CPAP. This time he was more demanding. The staff was concerned about Mark's rights; he had a choice about wearing this contraption. How could they make him? The suggestion was to try the behavioral specialist. The specialist was to be contacted to outline steps to work with Mark. We were told the process would begin soon. Once my brother began wearing the CPAP consistently, we hoped his health would improve. We planned to return with Mark during the summer to meet Dr. Rubin for a follow-up.

Mark had not been living in the group home for more than a few days when he lifted his arms up, hands out with palms up and proclaimed, "I love this place." It became his new mantra. Each time my parents, my sister, brothers, or myself visited, we could hear the public announcement, "I love this place." It's almost like he was reminding us, just in case we forgot, that he was happy living in the group home.

It takes a collaboration of interested individuals to make sure those with special needs have the best quality of life they can experience. Just as adults age and have increasing medical issues, those with special needs run into similar and even more complex medical and psychological problems. As family members we wanted the best for our loved one and appreciated the efforts of physicians and caregivers who took time to work with our family.

For whatever time he had left on this earth, our goal was for Mark Carroll Simpson to have a life of quality and happiness. I could visualize that when the time came for my brother to leave this world he would walk slowly through the gates of heaven smiling. And just as he checked the mailbox each time he walked through the door at the group home, he'd first check the heavenly mailbox to see if he had a letter. And of course, there would be a letter with celestial money in it.

The angels would then greet him applauding and waving. Mark would look around, introduce himself, shake a few hands, smile and proclaim,
"I love this place!"

The fabric of our lives is richer, the texture more diverse, the color palette more vibrant than those whose lives have not been touched by difference. Whether you are a parent, a teacher, a physician, a therapist or sibling, your life is enhanced by your belief in someone whose learning style is inherently different. Viva la difference!

Cynthia S. Kidder and Brian Skotko, "Band of Angels Press Survey" in Common Threads, Celebrating Life with Down Syndrome, Rochester Hills: Band of Angels Press, 2001, pg. 2. Reprinted with permission

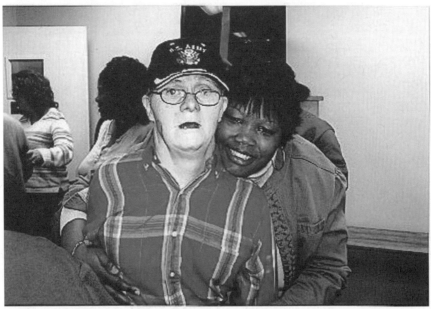

These photos of Mark with two of his favorite caregivers, Antwain and Cynthia.

Epilogue

As with too many governmental institutions, the red tape to procure a behavior specialist took a ridiculous length of time. After the consult with Dr. Rubin in November 2005, the behavior specialist finally called my sister in March of 2006 to work on a plan of behavior modification to help Mark with the wearing of his CPAP.

Unfortunately my brother's health began deteriorating at an alarming rate. His seizures worsened and became more frequent. The lack of oxygen getting into his body was extraordinarily low. Mark had a myriad of health issues.

After several days in the hospital, my brother was home for only one night before he became ill again and was re-admitted. The group home staff announced that at this time they could no longer care for Mark's medical needs. At least for a few months, my brother would have rehabilitation in a nursing facility.

Just days before we selected a nursing home, Mark relapsed.

My husband and I had flown to Virginia to help with the hospital stay and transition. The first morning of my visit was upbeat and Mark appeared to be responding to his medication and increased oxygen. He smiled lovingly at my mother as she helped feed him. He kept pointing to the balloons with smiley faces that I had brought, loving their bright yellow color that reminded him of sunshine. Mom and I were able to get him to walk outside his hospital room. We held on to him as he gingerly scooted around, waving at passersby.

We left Mark that afternoon sleeping and in good spirits. One of the group home staff was to come in later to check on him.

Clark and I returned at five o'clock to stay with Mark during his evening meal. As I walked into the room I couldn't believe my eyes. Mark was shaking severely; he was having a seizure! Immediately, I called the nurse and the next two hours became pure terror for me. Having little experience with hospitals, I felt totally helpless as I sat by my brother trying to understand what was happening. I helped the nurse hold Mark's arm as she found a vein to inject medication to help reduce the seizures. After the seizures subsided, he seemed to go into respiratory distress. I was terrified for my precious brother as the nurses tried to stabilize him. They had called the physician to return to the hospital. At seven o'clock he was taken to the critical care ward. Mark's physician in a straight forward, but gently voice said, "Call the family, I don't think Mark will make it." He explained that physiologically his body seemed to be shutting down.

The next eighteen hours appear now somewhat surreal. Our family rushed to the hospital. My sister-in-law, Nancy, with her medical expertise as a nurse anesthetist, became a godsend. In all those hours, she rarely left my brother's side. While the whirring and swooshing endless sounds of the CPAP machine drove me crazy, Nancy just accepted it, holding Mark's hand and gently talking to him. I think the first two hours Clark and I were alone with Mark had taken every last ounce of energy out of me. You could have picked me up like a washcloth and wrung me out. I was tense and exhausted. I didn't seem to have any more to give.

My sister, Dianna, sat on the other side of Mark's bed. She, too, had the patience of Job, being able to stay with Mark for such lengthy hours.

I walked in occasionally, one time speaking to Mark, kissing him on the forehead. Once I sat next to him holding his warm hand, he seemed so calm. Other times I would anxiously sit on a chair in the room, but it wasn't long and I would find myself heading back to the waiting area.

We sent my eighty-year-old parents home—it was just too much for them to bear. Mom did not want to leave, but we knew their health could not stand the possible long night ahead. It was the right decision.

I found I was more valuable saying prayers and talking with relatives and answering phones. When I was tired, I curled up and tried to sleep in the chairs... it didn't work.

The parish priest came for a final blessing. Several family members stood around the bed while Nancy and Dianna retained their watchful positions by Mark's side.

The breathing lessened, it was quieter, more peaceful.

It was close. The male nurse came in and someone made a comment about being so emotional.

"It's ok at a time like this," the male nurse said, "remember, even Jesus wept."

Dianna, realizing that Mark was so close to death, stood next to his head, bent over close to his face and began singing into Mark's ear, ever so softly, "Happy birthday to you, happy birthday to you."

Overcome with emotion I left the room. Knowing Mark's birthday was the following week and knowing how much he loved that song, Dianna sent Mark out on a happy note.

It was the most touching moment, one I will always hold dear. I wish I could have stayed in the room for the final prayer... I just fell apart.

At one-forty in the afternoon on Saturday, April 8, my brother, Mark Carroll Simpson, left this world, bound for a better place. A place where he would no longer have a disability, a place where there are no genetic conditions.

My mind recalled my husband's favorite poem from The Catholic Yearbook that begins, "Live each day to the fullest. Get the most from each hour, each day, and each age of your life." Mark was the epitome of that philosophy. He lived each day, enjoying each present moment, thinking little about the future. In his last days, he had no concept of death; therefore he had no fear.

The next days reminded me of Charle's Dickens oxymoron, "It was the best of times, it was the worst of times." The best was bringing our family closer than we had ever been; the worst was coping with this loss.

From Friday at five o'clock in the evening until Saturday at one-forty in the afternoon, my family experienced one of the most traumatic days of our lives. We had been fortunate to be together for only cheerful occasions. Now we had to deal with the death of one of our most treasured loved ones.

Leaving the hospital I felt the release of worry but not tension...I no longer had to stress about Mark suffering. Now, however, our family had to cope with the grieving process.

We worried about the effect of this loss on our parents. Being seventy-nine and eighty, life can be so fragile. Add to this the loss of their son, regardless of his age-it's simply unthinkable.

The small Gretna community wrapped their arms around my family. There was a parade of well-wishers quietly soothing my parents. They brought in homemade desserts, salads, fried chicken, casseroles, and breads. There was no one group who organized this outpouring of food, people just came to comfort and this was the one thing they knew that would be needed.

The presence of all six of Mark's siblings was self-evident, but I didn't expect the response from Mark's oldest nephews and nieces. Mom and Dad's eldest grandchildren were scattered all over the country; but there was no question as to IF they should come. They ALL made reservations immediately—from California, Illinois, North Carolina, Missouri, Massachusetss, Washington, D.C., they came. To them Mark was not an uncle, he was like their brother.

Everything happened so fast. The wake was Sunday evening, the day after Mark's death. It was an emotional roller coaster. When I first saw Mark in the casket, he looked ten years younger and through my tears, I smiled. He looked so peaceful. I kept thinking, *could it be that Mark is really dead?* Everything was cast in a giant fog.

Mark was wearing his suit along with one of his special Olympic medals. In his hand, a ball cap. That was so appropriate. At one time Mark had over SIXTY ball caps in his room!

In the other hand, someone had placed a dollar bill! Yep, another of his favorite things right in the coffin with him.

Leave it to my brother to gather a cross section of folks who in normal circumstances would never be together. Mark's friends transcended all intellects, all cultures, all socio-economic levels! Coming to the wake were people of all colors as well as those who farmed, those who taught, those who worked at factories, and those who were executives.

The highlight of the evening was watching Mark's group home buddies and staff come to say their goodbyes. Our family greeted each and every one. One girl in her wheelchair had a tear coming down her face as she was slowly wheeled past the casket.

I glanced over at Mark and noticed that one of the residents had carefully placed over his jacket buttons several small flowers. It was her tribute, a way of sending love to her friend. One of his favorite caregivers became so emotionally upset that she unabashedly cried out, almost falling over with emotional grief.

The morning of the funeral I awakened and began to pray, "Come Holy Spirit, fill the hearts of thy faithful." I needed strength to endure this day and this Catholic prayer seemed fitting. I wanted to be present to my parents who were having such a difficult time accepting the reality that their son was on longer on this earth.

Strangely, upon arrival at the church I felt a wave of peace come over me. I was no longer teary-eyed, no longer sad. It was dreamlike. I saw myself greeting people with complete composure. I was introduced to the group home staff and director. I thanked friends for coming. Could this be me? My prayer had been answered.

St. Victoria's, the little Catholic church on the hill, had dressed in her finest spring attire complete with blooming dogwoods, forsythia, and freshly mowed grass courtesy of Mark's twin cousins, John and Tom Reutter. Mark's beloved sunshine was abundant, a day ordered specifically for him.

The family was involved in all aspects of the funeral mass. My sister worked on the liturgy and sensitively involved the relatives. Pall bearers were nephews, readers were nieces, musicians were family friends. Even those who couldn't attend wanted in some way to be present. My sister-in-law, Suellen, had written a poem that fit so well, touching yet humorous. The priest was so welcoming and personable, explaining parts of the funeral mass to guests not familiar with the Catholic liturgy.

At the offertory, a basket of Mark's favorite things was brought up including his basketball, Special Olympic medals, McDonald's cup and Big Mac box, a ball cap, and his wallet. My brother, Chris, had written an explanation of each item and what it meant to Mark. This truly was a celebration of his life!

Toward the end of the liturgy when Father asked anyone who wished to come forward to honor Mark, I mustered enough courage to speak. I had a strong voice, although the night before my voice was barely audible! I began my eulogy by thanking those who had cared for and given Mark so much joy all his life. I closed by reading the last paragraph of this book which at the time was in the hands of my editor. I was proud when my daughters spoke as well as Jennifer, Mark's niece. They shared wonderful Mark moments.

When his caseworker came forward we were surprised but eager to hear her words. She asked all of Mark's caregivers to stand. Four rows stood. We immediately applauded in thanksgiving for their gift of service and love to Mark. She, too, told a Mark story, beginning by saying, "We worked FOR Mark." The emphasis was on FOR as we all knew Mark had a knack for manipulating us to get what he wanted.

The celebration of Mark's life ended at the grave site where his niece Jacqueline brought us to tears with her bagpipes as she played "Amazing Grace".

After a delicious lunch prepared by the church parishioners, the seven eldest grandchildren who had spent many happy years at the recreation center with Mark decided to revisit the pool that had since become dilapidated. They walked the grounds together pointing out various memorable spots and discovered a huge tree growing inside the old pool where they had once spent hours swimming. My daughter, Christin, told me that it reminded her of the movie "Field of Dreams" when James Earl Jones spoke the "they will come" speech: "It'll be as if they dipped themselves in magic waters. The memories will be so thick they'll have to brush them away from their faces." The pool was their "magic water" and the memories were thick as the cousins ended the visit with a group hug and quietly left.

The service was over, so with heavy hearts we drove down the winding country road that would never again bring Mark to share in our family gatherings. He was resting elsewhere, leaving us to mourn his passing.

Just being together... somehow that brought us solace. Usually at reunions, the family played games, joked, laughed. This day after the funeral, we simply basked in togetherness. We told Mark stories, laughed, ate, walked, fished, lounged. Whatever the activity, it was the being together that somehow brought us comfort.

My mother particularly experienced it from her three sisters who had traveled from Kansas City to be by her side. I felt it by just sitting, walking, or talking with my sisters (I had told Nancy that she officially had moved from sister-in-law to sister), my brothers, my daughters, and my husband.

We were almost giddy as we discovered that those who had left the day after the funeral found themselves calling home telling of another remembered Mark moment or just wanting to stay in touch with those still at the farm.

As the entire day's events ended, it hit me like a tsunami... I'd never again have the joy to dance and laugh with Mark. In that wave of sadness I felt I might drown in sorrow from all the tears. Our family must now enjoy Mark through the retelling of his delightfully rich stories over and over again. Then I recalled the rest of the prayer of the Holy Spirit: "send forth thy Spirit, that they may renew the face of the earth." I felt at peace.

Mark might have been the last child to leave home, but I'm sure he was the first to enter heaven, leaving us changed for the better. We are a more tolerant family, knowing that gifts come in all sizes, shapes, intellects. He left us a family in harmony, coming together to mourn and celebrate his life. We treasure the memories of our special brother and my parent's special child.

The flag on my parent's farm that Mark had saluted innumerable times was flown at half mast in his honor.

Appendix

Those "blessed" with Down syndrome are a blessing to others. Those with Downs make us put all things into perspective.
Those with Downs add more to the lives of those that are "normal."
Those with Downs show us that happiness does not come from material things or intelligent thoughts.

Those that carried Downs throughout their lives will leave the world missed more than those that were "normal."

John Duncan
Founder
The Rise School
Houston, Texas

For Siblings of Adults with Down Syndrome
(advice from my point of view)

Upon reflection of times spent with my brother, I rejoice that I took the time to make those special moments happen. Living so far from home made it more of a challenge to help with Mark. The three summers when I took him generated such fond memories which I so fondly now treasure. Don't let those moments pass you by! Here are some ideas you might try—whether you live close by or far away from your brother or sister with Down syndrome:

- Schedule visits to your home. Even it is only a few days, plan to have your sibling come to your home. Your children will benefit from getting to know and understand and love those who are different.
- Don't let transportation be a road block for visits. Perhaps another sibling can drive him or her to your home. Share the cost of a flight with your parents or other siblings. Even when Mark lived in the group home, I was determined to have him attend his nephew's wedding in Nashville. It took time to arrange, but my sister and I found a staff person willing to drive Mark and stay with him. Mark had such a good time and his caregiver, Cynthia, did too! We had no idea that was to be the last wedding he would attend.
- Celebrate! I wanted to host Mark's 50th milestone birthday. I was able to work from long distance getting invitations designed, printed, and mailed. Locating musicians and planning food preparation was done through phone conversations with my mother. The event was a huge success and Mark was clearly touched. His last party with the entire family was spent by celebrating my father's 80th birthday. We had such fun dancing the night away with Mark. Always include your special sibling in every family affair.

- Share the burden. My sister and I automatically took over responsibilities in finding Mark a home when Dad broke his hip. I wish now we would have worked harder at consulting our brothers. We made an assumption that since they didn't step up to help they were too busy or didn't care. The truth is that since we DID step up, they stepped back and let us do everything.
- Don't forget to take full advantage of the internet. When Mark became seriously ill, I decided one way to help was to become the main communicator for the family. After I spoke with my sister or mother, it became my job to relay to the rest of the family our brother's health status. My subject line was "Mark Update" and many relatives told me that when that subject popped up, they immediately opened the email. After creating a "family folder" of email addresses, it was easy to share news. Many family members conveyed their gratitude to me for keeping them so informed. Since Mark's death, no one wanted the family updates to stop. Mark has brought us closer as everyone is now updating the entire family on their individual activities. We've joked with one another via email, sent pictures of dog's birthdays, announced promotions, reminded each other to sing Happy Birthday to relatives, and even shared moments when we were feeling melancholy about Mark. The family updates have brought a new closeness that was not there before.
- Include grandchildren in caring for your loved one. After I began our family updates when Mark became ill, the response was so positive. For example, my daughter, Christin, who lives in Chicago, began putting Mark on her daytimer. Each month she religiously sent Mark a card with a dollar and photo inside (to help him remember her). She did this after I asked everyone to send Mark mail because he loved receiving cards and money in his daily checking of

the mail box. Here is what she wrote about three weeks after Mark's passing:

Hello Family,

Today my reminder to write Uncle Mark a card popped up. I opened up the reminder and deleted them all. I have been waiting for this day to come and today was it.

Wanted to share that with you. The loss of this Uncle will be the most difficult. Uncle Mark was really such a strong thread in the fabric of our family.

- Try to be involved with meetings concerning your special sibling. A friend of my parents who used to work at the sheltered workshop when Mark was there told me one suggestion she would make was to have the second generation (at least one sibling) as well as the first generation (the parents) be present at meetings. The family would have more people to ask questions and clearly understand any situation that need to be addressed. In addition, when aging care-givers were no longer able to help the adult with special needs, the siblings would better understand all aspects of the situation, including the history.
- When the transition is made from home to a group home or any new residence, keep a connection with your loved one. "You ARE your brother's keeper" even after the transition. For one thing, just like any sibling, the love for family is not changed just because one leaves home. Sisters and brothers desire to stay in touch with their families and enjoy periodic visits. It's critical for the mental health of the person with special needs to have continued interaction with loved ones. Don't just drop them at the door of their new home and forget to visit or include them in family activities. Visiting doesn't have to take much

time. Sometimes Mark was happy to see a family member for five or ten minutes. It was a brief "hello" that made him happy. My sister said there were times when she arrived at the group home Mark *"would be so happy and have those little tears in his eyes. It was touching."* One of my brothers was so emotional about the little time he had spent with Mark after he moved to the group home. The first thing he said to me at the hospital the night before our brother's death was, "I should have done more for Mark, I live close." I told him that at least he was there now, and his parents needed that support. He felt guilty and had a difficult time at the wake and funeral.

- Visit the home unannounced. My parents and my sister visited both the group home and the residential day-service (Mark went to day-service each week day where the residents enjoyed various activities and were transported to events in the community). They came all different times of the day to see Mark. The staff at both places welcomed my family's unannounced visits. Meeting and getting to know the staff who worked with my brother was an added advantage to the weekly visits. Occasionally my mother would bake homemade rolls for the entire staff. Each visit was relatively short, but Mark was always happy to see his family. Dad always gave Mark money; in return my brother gave his dad a military salute of thanks. Dianna many times would take Mark out to dinner at his favorite restaurant, McDonalds. "I come back here," he reminded her that he intended to go back to his beloved group home.
- Check on medications. We worked diligently to lessen medications that were given to Mark. At first, our brother had a gate-keeper physician that was not acceptable to our family. We simply did not feel he understood our brother. My sister knew a physician who was also a family friend and he was willing to

take Mark as his patient. The group home staff agreed to my sister's request. The problem came when Mark was taken to other specialists (neurologist, psychologist, sleep specialist, heart specialist, etc.). Unless his primary physician knew about the medications prescribed, my poor brother might have drugs that were interacting negatively in his body, making him at times seem to be like a zombie. Adding all his medications to his sleep apnea, there were days when he barely could stand and slept sitting up. Much of the problem was alleviated when all the specialists communicated first with his primary physician. Mark's medical issues were complicated and balancing his medications to give him a quality life was challenging. His primary physician worked hard to find that balance. It was the family, however, who kept questioning and prodding to get the caregivers to improve Mark's health. Don't accept a physician's diagnosis with blind faith. Ask questions and make sure doctors and caregivers understand the complex issues of people with Down syndrome. Most people, regardless of the number of degrees, DON'T!

- Work WITH the caregivers, not AGAINST them. Our family worked very hard to be understanding of Mark's caregivers. We understood there were times when Mark could be difficult to handle. He could be stubborn and belligerent. Mark was a gentle spirit, but because he could not articulate his concerns and frustrations, he did occasionally misbehave. We realized that some medication might be needed—we simply didn't want Mark to be so medicated that he was lethargic. There were times when he could barely get the hamburger he was eating from the plate to his mouth. Working with the group home and his physicians, we were able to resolve the problem with a change in medication. I think that if my family had yelled or been unkind, his caregivers would have been less willing to work with us.

- Check with the nurse frequently to make sure he or she is communicating with the gate-keeping physician. There were times when his primary physician was not even aware that Mark was in the emergency room; in fact, one ER doctor tripled Mark's dosage of a seizure medication. His primary physician was not cognizant of this—the triple dose for Mark could have been lethal.
- Try to include the people living and working at the group home or residence in your celebrations. My mother would bring a cake for everyone at the group home to share in Mark's birthday party. She also collected stuffed animals throughout the year from stores and garage sales, giving everyone a stuffed animal at Easter.

Internet Links I Found Helpful

www.ds-health.com – This web site is an excellent directory of organized sites to help find information about Down syndrome from all over the United States and the world. Once you get to the site, scroll down and click on "DS sites on the internet." You will be surprised how many sites are listed.

www.ndss.org – I found the National Down Syndrome Society web site to have a wealth of information. It's easy to peruse and includes up-to-date research and news.

www.ndsccenter.org- This is the site of the National Down Syndrome Congress. Their web site is particularly inviting. I phoned the congress a number of times and found the folks there to be good listeners and very caring. If they can't find an answer for you, they will guide you to someone who can.

www.disabilitysolutions.org- This site is a resource for families and all those interested in learning more about Down syndrome and other related disabilities. I found a number of articles helpful.

www.bandofangels.com- This is such a joyful website! If I were to meet a family who had a new baby with Down syndrome, one of the first places I would direct them would be to this site. It is so upbeat, so hopeful, so positive! On their home page they say, "We want the world to see not the differences, but the sameness of children with Down syndrome."

http://www.uic.edu/orgs/rrtcamr/SCresource.html- On November 9 and 10, 2007, the first National Sibling Leadership Network Conference was held in Washington, D.C. I was fortunate to attend this conference where siblings, service providers, policymakers and researchers came together to learn and converse about issues in an effort to help siblings of those with developmental disabilities. The conference attendees came away with a plan of action and began developing three white papers on sibling advocacy issues, policy recommendations, and a research agenda. Check out this website. It's a work in progress, but will eventually be a tremendous asset to siblings seeking information and support. Also, look for emerging state level chapters of the Sibling Leadership Network!

www.brookwoodcommunity.org- After visiting Brookwood near Houston this summer, I am still reeling over this unbelievable community for older Americans with disabilities. The founder, Yvonne Streit, is one of the most exciting, amazing women I've met. Although Yvonne is over eighty years old, she continues to be an incredible force that helps the community grow and is a vision of hope for so many. Anyone researching possibilities for a residential community for the disabled, you've got to check out this site. Not only is this place beautiful, it is a vibrant working community. Never say one person can't do much, just check out this website and realize that it just took one person and her vision— Yvonne Streit is truly inspirational and so is Brookwood!

www.dsah.net- This website has a wealth of information and stays current. The Down Syndrome Association of Houston site includes data that people from any state can use. I especially found their newsletters particularly informative. Newsletters are archived on the site.

www.misericordia.com- For another example of an outstanding place that helps those with developmental disabilities, take a look at Misericordia. The Mission of Misericordia (Heart of Mercy) is "to support individuals with developmental disabilities in maximizing their level of independence and self-determination within an environment that fosters spirituality, dignity, respect and enhancement of quality of life. We promote development of natural family and community support, community awareness, education and advocacy." Located in Chicago, Misericordia has a wide range of programs including job opportunities for adults with disabilities. I heard the bakery is wonderful and you can even purchase goodies online! I've been told that Director Sr. Rosemary Connelly gives Misericordia its heart. After having spoken with her briefly, I concur!

www.riseschool.org- I toured the Rise School of Houston with its founder, John Duncan, and discovered an excellent model for schools of young children with developmental disabilities! The spirit in this school is amazing and the results are impressive. Students are going on to elementary schools and doing exceptionally well. Check out the website to learn more about the fast expanding Rise schools!

My Favorite Books

Medical Care for Children & Adults with Developmental Disabilities, *Second Edition, 2006, I. Leslie Rubin, M.D., Allen C. Crocker, M.D, Paul H. Brookes Publishing Co., 2006*

I met Dr. Rubin in November just before his book was published. Being so impressed with such a caring physician, I bought it as soon as it was in print. The book is huge, packed with information concerning a variety of disabilities. I consulted the text numerous times when Mark became ill. It helped in my quest to better understand the more complex medical issues surrounding those with Down syndrome.

Common Threads, Celebrating Life with Down Syndrome, *Cynthia S. Kidder and Brian Skotko, Photography by Kendra Dew, Band of Angels Press, 2006*

This could be a coffee table book! The upbeat nature of the text and beautifully sensitive photos put a celebratory face on those with Down syndrome and with the wonderful successful stories, it's full of hope!

Another Season, A Coach's Story of Raising an Exceptional Son, *Gene Stallings and Sally Cook, Little, Brown and Company,1997*

This inspirational story of Johnny Stahlings and his family is a love lesson in father/son relationships. I was particularly interested in the book because Mark was ten years older than Johnny. The personality of Johnny was a fond remembrance of my brother. Johnny has had exceptional experiences with his father, a former football coach of the University of Alabama.

Laying Community Foundations for Your Child with a Disability, How to Establish Relationships That Will Support Your Child after You're Gone, *Linda J. Strengle, M.H.S., Woodbine House, 1996*

I feel this book has some excellent suggestions when considering future care-givers. Some families are small or relatives are non-existent. The author's focus is on developing volunteer advocates for your loved one with a disability. I know several adults with disabilities who have caring people within their organization who are advocates for them. One is the staff of a local YMCA and another is a church. The key is to begin developing these relationships early.

Mental Wellness in Adults with Down Syndrome, Dennis McGuire and Brian A. Chicoine, MD, Woodbine House, 2006

Oh, if only this book had been available during my brother's adult years, we would have been able to understand and better cope with all the idiosyncrasies common to many with Down syndrome. This book comes from two knowledgeable professionals who gained a lot of wisdom through working with adults with Down syndrome at their center in Park Ridge, Illinois. They share what they gathered from serving over 3,000 patients! In my opinion, every family, every caregiver, every friend of anyone who knows an adult with Down syndrome should have this book as a reference to go to whenever they don't understand the actions of their loved one with special needs. The answer is usually found there, as well as ideas to help with a solution.

In Remembrance

Dear Mark

By Sueellen Simpson
(Mark's sister-in-law)

When we think of you, what we'll remember the most,
Are the famous phrases you so often spoke.
We remember you saying and saying it well,
"wooda, wooda, baseball bat".
We thought that was swell.
And then on days that were spent with you,
You said, "Californian, California",
Where the skies are blue.
To avoid drinking water,
You'd try this trick,
You'd say, "I hate water!
Water makes me sick!"
And often on days that were filled with rain,
We heard you say it again and again,
"thunderstorms, thunderstorms, I hate thunderstorms!"
When the weather was nice, on beautiful days,
Your words rang out, we heard you say,
"Sunshine, sunshine! I love sunshine!"
And now you are where the water is fine.
It won't make you sick, for it is simply divine.
And where you are now,
For this we're so sure,"thunderstorms, thunderstorms"
are no more.
You've been called home,
We know this is true,
Where everlasting "sunshine, sunshine" is shining down
on you.
And when we meet again,
face to face,
we'll hear you say,
"I love this Place"

Read by Chris Simpson (Mark's brother)
Mark's Mass of the Resurrection
Monday, April 10, 2006

Mark – Intelligence of the Heart

Caroline Baker

As the daughter of the eldest Simpson child, I was lucky to experience so many wonderful times when Mark was in his prime.

I will never forget coming to Gretna, and always being welcomed by Grandma, Grandpa, and a hug from Uncle Mark that would always squeeze the breath out of me.

They say that people with Down syndrome have the "Intelligence of the heart", and isn't Mark a poster child for that statement?

I want to thank Mark, sincerely, from the bottom of my heart, because without him, I would not be the woman I am today. You may think I am kidding, but that's the truth. And I am not talking about being sensitive towards people with disabilities, I am talking about where I am today with my education, my job, and what I do on a daily basis.

Mark helped me get into both of my colleges. I wrote both of my essays about him and growing up with him as a major influence on my life.

My second career choice was to be a special education teacher, because I was fascinated with Mark and educating people with disabilities. I always remember Mark saying, "Gimme a job, Gimme a job, Gimme a job," and that's what he helped me do... get a job! I am in my third year teaching special education, and I would not be doing that if it weren't for him.

I remember when Uncle Mark used to go on road trips with Jean Paul and Daniel (his nephews), they would try to teach him the months of the year. They would start with January, February, and so on. Mark would always go from January to April... he could never remember any other month than April! I think it's so beautiful that God brought Mark into this world in April (the twenty-third) and he left us almost fifty-four years later—in April. He really loves April!

I could go on for a long time, just as everyone has done, telling stories and experiences with my uncle, but I want to leave you with a list of the philosophy of life Mark lived by:

1. Do your job to the fullest, going above and beyond the call of duty, even if it means digging massive holes when told to make one hole for a fence post.
2. Always say "please", "thank you", and "I am sorry" for everything.
3. Jumping in the pool at the YMCA in your underwear is completely acceptable, and so much fun.
4. If you want to sneak something, the best hiding places are: in your pocket, because no one could notice a coke there, behind the toilet, or under the deck.
5. Take long showers, as long as you can, and always lock the bathroom door so no one can tell you to get out.
6. If you feel like spitting, don't hold back, but just don't spit on the floor... simply use your hand for that kind of stuff.
7. Sing as loud as you can and play instruments even if you don't know how.
8. Watch you money... don't let it go easily, but really think about every purchase as you are making it.
9. Dance until you can't even stand up! AND LASTLY
10. Love everyone unconditionally, with all your heart.

Eulogy delivered
By Caroline Baker (Mark's niece)
Mark's Mass of the Resurrection
Monday, April 10, 2006

What I Learned From Uncle Mark

Jennifer Murphy
(Mark's eldest niece)

As I was thinking about memories of Uncle Mark, I realized I learned a lot from him and it's more than where Granny hides the Coke.

—I learned how to swim all the away across the Simpson's Recreation Center pool from the deep end to the shallow end (7 feet to 3 inches) without touching the bottom.

—I learned the ceremonial head flip at the end of that swim to get hair out of my face.

—I learned how to sweep sand in water with minimal clouding.

—I learned that there are bears in Motley... and that they are white.

But—there is more than that. I learned:

Perseverance— Never give up despite what people say. As a young child I saw Uncle Mark learn how to roller skate when people told him he wouldn't be able to walk.

Set Goals and Reach for a Dream—"Four more years" says it all. My husband, Sean and I donated to the Special Olympics in Uncle Mark's honor.

Gratitude—Always say "Thank you, Thank you very much." It didn't matter what you did for Uncle Mark, he was always appreciative.

Animation—Telling a story is good but it is always better with hand gestures.

Joy— Be Happy to See People— Whenever you walked through the door, he was always happy to see you (even if you just came back from the grocery store). Every time you visited, he wanted to make sure you came back.

Jennifer sent this reflection on the one month Anniversary of Mark's death

Jennifer (joined by her mother, Nancy) rode 431 miles across
North Carolina in six days in honor of her Uncle Mark.

Reflections from the Grave Site

Mark's sister, Dianna Lavoie

I had my solo gathering with Mark today at his grave site, celebrating his birthday which would have been this weekend, April 23, 2006.

It was hard to go. It was the first time I visited since the funeral a mere week ago. After being there while, however, I found it hard to leave. It was like just after he died and I did not want to leave him! I know it's a shell of a body, but there is something about being there. I do feel Mark's presence all the time but it was stronger today.

While Nancy and I were with Mark we wondered what he would have been like had he not had Down syndrome. Carolyn gave me that answer the other day when she said he needs red, white and blue near his grave because he was so patriotic. I suddenly realized that Mark would have been in the military, just like his Dad. He loved the army and I pictured this ever so handsome young man saluting the flag for his country. So I went to the store and bought a little plaque that was red, white and blue and spelled out USA. I purchased two American flags and brought them to his grave. I also brought him a Dr. Pepper and gently placed it in the basket mom had placed there. I know he loved it.

I sat and talked to Mark at the grave for awhile. Mom had brought up two balloons— one with a big smiley face and another with a more feminine look to it. When I arrived at the grave site they were pretty much laying down, but when I began to talk to Mark and place my items on his grave they perked up. As I sat down the one big smiley face turned toward me and looked straight at me as if it was taking in every word I said.

I asked out loud, "Mark, what are you doing up there?"

The smiley face turned toward the other feminine-looking balloon and the two balloons begin to flow together as if dancing. The smaller balloon kept snuggling up to the big smiley face. I believe that Mark was telling me that he had a girlfriend and they were dancing. As along as I can remember, Mark wanted a girlfriend and had one in Germany. And now I just sense that this is one thing Mark has, a true love all to himself and she loves him with all her heart.

There was so little wind out and yet these balloons were dancing and so is our Mark. I didn't want to leave, but I did so with a vision of Mark dancing with this incredibly sweet woman at his side!

I did leave realizing that I need to go to the place where his body is— just to be.

The hospital called my parents over six months after Mark's death about an item they found that belonged to him (including clothing minus his brand new shoes). The experience of coming to retrieve his wallet could have/should have been a positive, caring moment for the hospital. Instead, it was done with haste and little sensitively toward their loss. May we all try to be more considerate when we encounter those who have experienced a loss in their family.

The Wallet

A wallet was found.
It was unique with a long, fat silver chain attached.
People at the hospital seemed not to care...
They see death each day
and besides
It hadn't belonged to THEIR uncle,
It hadn't belonged to THEIR brother,
It hadn't belonged to THEIR son...
BUT
It was OUR uncle's wallet..
It was OUR brother's treasure..
It was THEIR son's favorite possession.
Mom and Dad were handed Mark's wallet
Just yesterday...
by a noncaring, nonchalant employee....
who didn't notice the treasures within...
the two one dollar bills...
the two lottery tickets....
the photograph.
From my brother's wallet the photo was gingerly
pulled from inside,
it was of his parents.
Mark had only his Mom and Dad's picture in
with what he loved.

As they gazed at the items Mom and Dad couldn't
help it,
They cried.
Don't cry, Mom.
Don't cry, Dad.
Mark doesn't need that wallet anymore.
He's left it behind...
He's in a place where he has a better wallet
with more money than he'll ever need...
He's probably scratching a ticket right now..
And that photo...
Well, it's in his heart...
Don't you feel his spirit!
He's with us in many ways each day...
Sending you love and kisses...
and every time you win with a lottery ticket..
don't think it's coincidence!
It's Mark...
touching your heart...
touching our hearts.
What comfort came from finding one simple
wallet.

A light moment with Mark and his sisters.

Acknowledgements

"Hey, do you have any more Mark stories?"
"What's going on with Mark nowadays?"
"These are stories to treasure, you need to put them in writing."

When I realized how many friends and relatives loved hearing about Mark, his unique personality and his entertaining adventures, a seed was planted within me. This seed slowly began to grow and eventually sprouted a desire to write a book about Mark's adult life. As years went by and our family had to work through trials and tribulations of Mark's journey and his desire to leave home as well as his mounting medical problems, I recognized that this book could be more than a treasury of stories. It actually could one day help other families who might be going through a similar situation.

It all began with friends, family, and co-workers at Overbrook School in Nashville, Tennessee, who helped to plant this seed. In particular, my book club (which began while at Overbrook), brought about a new desire to write. Being introduced to a variety of authors and realizing that we all have a story to tell, I began to gain confidence, seriously considering to pen a book about my brother.

Then we moved. My husband had an opportunity to be the CEO of the YMCA of Houston, Texas. This change introduced me to something I wasn't used to... time!

Noticing that Rice University was offering a class on writing the nonfiction book, I signed up, realizing this was an opportunity that might guide me in my new endeavor. That's when Elizabeth Harper Neeld came into my life. Elizabeth, the instructor, had written 17 books and her incredible upbeat, vibrant spirit jump-started my writing. Elizabeth continues to coach me—even with her busy schedule, she has continued to correspond with me and has been one of the most influential people in my writing life.

Another instructor, Alexis Glynn Latner, taught "Shaping Your Story," and was willing to read a number of chapters from my manuscript, giving me constructive criticism. I would recommend the Rice University Continuing Education Program to anyone!

Elizabeth encouraged our class to form a writing community. Through this process, I met Rufi Natarajan. We became writing partners and sat for hours at a favorite restaurant sharing our written projects. I gratefully acknowledge Rufi as she was one of the first to support completion of my book. Another person who, although did not know me, took time to read a few chapters and make suggestions was Sue Joe from the National Down Syndrome Congress. The people I spoke with each time I called were so kind and considerate.

I also appreciate the willingness of those authors whose work I referenced at the beginning and end of each chapter. Their permission to use the quotes will help individuals who read this book better understand those with special needs.

I will be forever indebted to Dr. Rubin who was so valuable to us in those last months of Mark's life. Dr. Rubin took the time to read my manuscript and write the foreword to this writing. This man, who is so respected in his field and so incredibly busy, took time out of his schedule to respond to a novice writer. His gentle spirit and encouragement came into my life when I needed someone to say, "Hey, you've got a good story here." The world needs more people like him and his kind staff at the Adult Down Syndrome Center in Atlanta, Georgia.

The other physician I want to thank is Dr. Stewart Sharp who kindly accepted Mark as his patient. He was an answer to our prayers when we became frustrated with the impersonal care he was getting from other physicians.

While I was gathering information, I had help from Rena Howard, Director of Mental Retardation Services for the Danville-Pittsylvania Community Services. I appreciate her efforts to help with my book as well as Mark's case worker, Connie Chappell, and Corene Hermanson (residential services director). Thanks to all those day care group home employees who loved my brother and were so kind to him. One of Mark's caregiver's, Cynthia Hutchinson, even crafted a charming scrapbook honoring Mark, presenting it to my parents as a special memory of her friend.

My editor, Kendal Gladish, is not only an excellent content specialist, but a kind, caring, sensitive woman who has been like a guiding beam of light during this entire process.

I also want to thank John Duncan who read my manuscript and was so positive, it gave me the momentum to keep working on getting this thing published!
I had to be so trusting as I am a novice to the book business. I found that someone with my layout designer, Layne Moore. I immediately sensed that this was an honorable man who could guide me through the publishing aspect of the writing process. Thanks to him for patiently steering me in the right direction.

Several people who were important in my story include Bob Copeland and Mark Weller from the YMCA Joe C. Davis Center, in Nashville. Thanks for providing fantastic summers for Mark. Special thanks to his counselors, in particular, Dan Schlacter and John King. David Read from the YMCA gave life to my cover, which he sensitively designed. Early on, Pam Beaver read a few chapters, gave me solid encouragement, and even offered marketing ideas. Patty Donbeck, a book club member and dear friend, read my manuscript and provided encouragement to keep me going. Thanks, too, to David and Marjorie Snow for welcoming Mark each time he visited us in Nashville. Marjorie would always tease Mark about being the same age. I appreciate their support for my project. Random acts of kindness can be so meaningful and the special card I received after the death of my brother from the students and teacher at the Hand in Hand Program at Pope John Paul II High School meant so much to me. All the students in this program have Down syndrome and to receive a card from them at this time touched me and made me realize that I needed to get back to the goal of publishing this book

My family has been so important to *Last To Leave Home*. My daughter's, Christin and Caroline, have been my cheerleaders. It's been a long process, their unwavering belief in me has never faltered. I am grateful to my parents for allowing me to write this story that is so close to their hearts. They have never questioned what I've written, they just have had faith in my work. To my brothers and their wives, thanks for supporting me and especially for being so good to Mark. Christopher, your idea for the title of my book has made all the difference. That title says it all in a nutshell. A special thanks to Jean Paul Lavoie, Mark's nephew, for being the webmaster for my book. You alleviated much of my stress by accepting this task! Also, I appreciate the writings found in the remembrance section by Dianna Lavoie, Jennifer Murphy, Sueellen Simpson, and my daughter, Caroline. Other family members not previously mentioned, but who played important roles in Mark's story include Allan Lavoie (Mark's brother-in-law), Megan Simpson and Jacqueline Lavoie (Mark's nieces), Daniel Lavoie (Mark's nephew), and Nancy Simpson (Mark's sister-in-law).

My sister, Dianna, has inspired me to write just by her actions. She generously gives to others and her commitment to Mark was a story I wanted to tell.

My faith has been woven throughout this process. Every time I sat down to write, I would pray to the Holy

Spirit for inspiration. He didn't let me down! I want to thank the Dominican Sisters in Nashville, Tennessee, for their encouragement. Each time I bumped into the sisters they would inquire about my book and have been a spiritual support for me. Another rock of faith for me has been Clark's aunt, Sr. Frances Joan Baker. Sister's never ending prayers and uplifting spirit has helped me in all aspects of my life... not just writing.

Last, but not least, my husband, Clark, who kept encouraging me. Whenever, I was frustrated, he would say, "Don't worry, take your time. You have a self-imposed deadline, you can take as long as you wish." Thanks for being there for me—a hug, a phone call, a smile, and an Irish coffee now and again were blessings during this whole process.

Of course, it goes without saying, that I want to thank my dearest brother, Mark. This man taught me that it doesn't take intelligence to make the world a better place, it takes love. Mark inspired all of us to become better citizens and to enjoy each moment of each day. My dear brother, you were the last to leave home, but you will never leave our hearts. We treasure the memories. This book is written totally out of love for you and totally in your honor.

Mark sits on the lap of his father in an early family photo.

The Final Salute

This military gesture was made as Mark greeted his father from the hospital bed for the last time. My brother was patriotic and respectful till the very end of his life.

About the cover...

This photograph was taken around 1954 when our father was a young soldier and mom was busy raising four children. At that time little was known about Down syndrome. Dad's decision to keep Mark at home, which was not recommended by many in the medical field, was life changing for Mark, as well as for our family. My parents accepted and embraced the fact that Mark may never be able to leave home.